SOMERSET
THE MILLENNIUM BOOK

Edited by
Tom Mayberry & Hilary Binding

With a Foreword by
HRH the Prince of Wales

Somerset Books

SOMERSET ARCHAEOLOGICAL &
NATURAL HISTORY SOCIETY

First published in 1999 by Halsgrove
Copyright © Somerset Archaelogical and Natural History Society
Somerset County Council and the Authors

ISBN 0 86183 485 2

British Library Cataloguing-in-Publication-Data
A CIP data record for this book is available from the British Library

SOMERSET BOOKS
Halsgrove House
Lower Moor Way
Tiverton EX16 6SS
T: 01884 243242
F: 01884 243325
www.halsgrove.com

Printed and bound in United Kingdom
by WBC Ltd, Bridgend

CONTENTS

CONTRIBUTORS

Sue Berry is Senior Archivist and Education Officer at the Somerset Record Office.

Dr Joe Bettey retired recently as Reader in Local History at the University of Bristol.

Hilary Binding is a freelance historian, writer and editor, and Vice Chairman of the Somerset Archaeological and Natural History Society.

Robin Bush is a writer, lecturer and broadcaster. He was formerly Deputy County Archivist for Somerset, and also served as Assistant Editor of the *Victoria County History*.

Dr Michael Costen is Staff Tutor in Historical Studies at the Centre for the Historic Environment, University of Bristol.

Dr Robert Dunning is Somerset Editor of the *Victoria County History* and Chairman of the Somerset Archaeological and Natural History Society.

Tom Mayberry is Assistant County Archivist at the Somerset Record Office and former editor of the *Proceedings* of the Somerset Archaeological and Natural History Society.

Mary Siraut is Assistant Editor for Somerset of the *Victoria County History*.

Professor David Underdown is Professor of History, Emeritus, at Yale University.

A NOTE ON THE ILLUSTRATIONS

The watercolours with which this volume is chiefly illustrated are held by the Somerset Archaeological and Natural History Society and form part of an unsurpassed visual record of the county during the first half of the nineteenth century. Most of the watercolours are contained in two large collections. The Pigott Collection was commissioned by John Hugh Smyth-Pigott, FSA (*c* 1792–1853), of Brockley Hall and of Grove House, Weston super Mare. It consists of six large volumes containing 1,154 wash drawings entitled 'Illustrations of the Ecclesiastical and Domestic Architecture of Somerset...' The artists were John Buckler, FSA (1770–1851), and his son John Chessell Buckler (1793–1894). Smyth-Pigott's drawings were bequeathed to the county of Somerset, placed at Quarter Sessions under trustees, and deposited by them with the Society, which has retained them ever since.

The Braikenridge Collection (or rather collections, as there are parallel ones covering Bristol in Bristol Central Library and Bristol City Art Gallery) was formed by George Weare Braikenridge, FSA, FGS (1775–1856), of Broomwell House, Brislington. His Somerset collection originally took the form of an extra-illustrated copy of John Collinson's *History and Antiquities of Somerset* (1791) enlarged from three to fourteen volumes by the addition of prints and watercolours. The majority of the watercolours were commissioned from William Walter Wheatley (1811–1885) and Samuel Griffiths Tovey (1808–1873), though a number of other better-known artists are also represented, including Francis Danby, Samuel Jackson, T.L.S. Rowbotham, John Inigo Richards and Edward Dayes. On the death of G.W. Braikenridge the Somerset collection passed to his son William Jerdone Braikenridge, and on the latter's death in 1907 it was bequeathed to the Society.

David Bromwich
Honorary Librarian, SANHS

ACKNOWLEDGEMENTS

For help in bringing this book to publication the editors are particularly grateful to David Cawthorne, Steven Pugsley, Dr Robert Dunning, Keith Jackson and Adam Green. Generous help has also been received from David Dawson, Stephen Minnitt, Bob Croft, Chris Webster and Janet Tall, and a particular debt is owed to David Bromwich for his expert guidance through the illustrative collections of the Somerset Archaeological and Natural History Society. Other help in describing illustrations and making them available has kindly been provided by Brian McCulloch, Paula Lewis, the late Mrs Ina Payne, Sheena Stoddard, Michaela Parker, Philip Marke, Martin Michell and Tony Steddall. Photography was undertaken by Lawrence Bostock of the County Museums Service, Richard Sainsbury of Delmar Studios, QPC Photography, and Peter Collings of the Somerset Archive and Record Service. Conservation was undertaken by Mervyn Richens of the Archive and Record Service. The book was designed by Karen Binaccioni.

The majority of the illustrations, including all those in colour, are reproduced from the collections of the Somerset Archaeological and Natural History Society. For permission to use other illustrations the following are gratefully acknowledged: Mr and Mrs V.H. Alford, p. 134; Ashmolean Museum, Oxford, p. 15 (right); Bristol Museums and Art Gallery, p. 84; P.E. Collings, p. 26 (below); Dr Michael Costen, p. 17 (below); Mr and Mrs L.A.J. Dicks, p. 110; Enmore Primary School, p. 109; Mrs Iris Groves, p. 130; T.W. Mayberry, pp. 24, 89, 128, 129, 139; Somerset Archive and Record Service, pp. 60, 82, 83, 90, 91, 106, 108, 113, 118, 121, 122, 127, 131, 132, 135, 136; Somerset County Museums Service, pp. 12, 17 (above); Somerset Cricket Museum, 137; *Western Daily Press*, p. 138.

FOREWORD

ST. JAMES'S PALACE

More than eleven hundred years have passed since Alfred the Great, threatened with the loss of his kingdom, left his refuge on the Isle of Athelney and defeated the Danes at the Battle of Edington. The chroniclers tell us that 'all the people of Somerset' rallied to the king at that fateful time and, since then, as this new book records, Somerset has often had its place in national history. Local men such as Sir Matthew de Gournay (whose Somerset lands were acquired by my predecessors as Dukes of Cornwall) fought for the Black Prince in the Hundred Years War. Others played a leading part in the tragic conflicts of the seventeenth century; and it was Somerset that sheltered the young Charles II as he escaped into exile after the Battle of Worcester.

Somerset's wonderful medieval buildings, including the cathedral at Wells - for which I have a very special personal affection - and its many fine parish churches, are for me the most vivid reminders of the county's long history. I am delighted that this splendidly-illustrated book will make more of that history readily available. The book also marks the 150th anniversary of the Somerset Archaeological and Natural History Society which, with Somerset County Council, has made publication of this volume possible. It is particularly timely that this history appears as the second millennium draws to a close, a time which inspires us not only to look to the future, but also to remember and celebrate the richness of our past.

INTRODUCTION

Somerset is one of the most diverse of English shires. The ancient county reaches from the borders of Bristol in the north, to Yeovil in the south-east and Dulverton in the west, and gathers in the bleakly impressive Mendip Hills, the levels of central Somerset, the fertile soils in the south of the county, and the highlands of the far west. It was the Anglo-Saxons who first gave geographical identity to this disparate territory, and it is a remarkable fact that Somerset, together with other shires of the former kingdom of Wessex, is older than England itself, and far older than any state of mainland Europe.

Somerset's landscape, and the story of the people who have shaped it to their needs, are the subject of the essays this book contains. The essays have been written by nine Somerset historians, and cover such major themes as the origins of the shire, its agricultural exploitation from the Middle Ages onwards, the rise of towns and gentry families, the disasters of civil war and rebellion, and the transforming changes of the nineteenth and twentieth centuries.

The book has a dual purpose. It summarises more than one thousand years of county history as the second millennium draws to a close and also marks the 150th anniversary of the Somerset Archaeological and Natural History Society. Since its foundation in 1849 the Society has been a leading promoter of research and publication in the county, as well as an outstanding collector of sources relating to Somerset. The Society's archaeological collections form the basis of the County Museum at Taunton Castle; its archives include some of the greatest treasures preserved in the Somerset Record Office; and its library, together with the County Council's Somerset Studies Library, is one of the richest sources of printed local history in any English county. The Society also possesses an unsurpassed collection of Somerset illustrations, and the publication of this book provides a welcome opportunity to give prominence to a small selection of them. They include not only historically important watercolours by W.W. Wheatley, S.G. Tovey and the Bucklers, father and son, but works by leading artists of the Bristol School such as Francis Danby and Samuel Jackson.

Many people have contributed to the making of this book. In particular, thanks are due to the officers of the Somerset Archaeological and Natural History Society for their enthusiastic support, as well as to the Publications Liaison Group of Somerset County Council.

Adam Green
County Archivist

THE MAKING OF
THE SHIRE

1

THE MAKING OF THE SHIRE

Michael Costen

The traditional date for the coming of the Anglo-Saxons (the English) to the territory they called Somerset is usually given as AD 658. In that year the *Anglo-Saxon Chronicle* records that the Anglo-Saxon king of Wessex, Cenwalh, fought the native Welsh at 'Pen' and 'drove them in flight as far as the Parrett'. We shall return to the English later, but first we must look at the region before their arrival. Who lived here? How did they live? And what was their society like?

The Old Welsh inhabitants of the region during the fifth to seventh centuries were descendants of the Romano-British population. They seem to have organised their society around chieftains, and perhaps kings, who dominated an area approximating to that of the later county. To the north the boundary was probably marked by the line of Wansdyke, while on the east, the thickly-wooded area later called the Forest of Selwood made a good natural frontier. The great Iron Age hillfort at South Cadbury, Cadbury Castle, was re-fortified on a lavish scale in this period. Over 20,000 metres of timber went into the ramparts and a large hall stood on the top-most part of the hill. This was indeed a site fit for a king (though probably not the mythical King Arthur), and may have served as a political and military centre dominating the whole of central Somerset.

Elsewhere, traces of great estates ruled by nobles can probably be discerned. At Cannington, for example, the hillfort has produced evidence of a large cemetery which was in use from late Roman times until the late seventh or early eighth century. Professor Philip Rahtz, the excavator of the site, recovered 523 graves but estimated that there may have been as many as 5,000 before the hill was quarried away. The later burials were certainly Christian. The presence of so many graves suggests that the catchment area for the cemetery was quite large, certainly larger than the settlement at Cannington itself. I have suggested elsewhere that the cemetery served an estate which covered the whole of the Cannington region from the River Parrett in the east to the sea on the north-west and having the Quantock Hills as its southern boundary. Other great estates may have been centred on Brent Knoll, Cadbury–Congresbury, the hilltop site at Lamyatt Beacon, Banwell or its neighbourhood, and Wells. Cadbury Castle and Cadbury–Congresbury have both yielded pottery from the Mediterranean as evidence of some degree of long-distance trade, possibly controlled from aristocratic sites such as these. Other centres of power may also have existed, but they cannot be identified as yet.

Cadbury Castle, South Cadbury, after a drawing by the antiquary William Stukeley, 1723.

What did not exist were towns. The old Roman towns at Ilchester, Camerton and Charlton near Shepton Mallet had fallen into decay in the fifth century and while Bath, far to the north, may have survived late into the fifth century as a semi-urban site, it was to become linked with the Anglo-Saxon kingdoms of the Midlands and did not return to Somerset until the time of Alfred the Great. The sparse evidence suggests that pastoral farming played a significant part in the landscape and that arable farming was restricted to those areas which were close to important centres. How many inhabitants there were we cannot tell. In common with much of western Europe the region may have seen a drastic decline in population during the fifth century. Nevertheless the Old Welsh, on the eve of the Anglo-Saxon conquest, possessed a well-organised society with a hierarchy of aristocracy and peasants. Theirs was also a Christian society and had been, at least among the powerful, since the fourth century.

*

Silver amulet cross, decorated with a Christian chi-rho monogram, found in a grave of the late fourth or early fifth century at Foss Lane, Shepton Mallet, 1990.

The Anglo-Saxons not only gave Somerset a name, but also established for it a geographical identity which was to remain largely unchanged for more than a thousand years. There is no good reason to doubt the tradition that they took over the region in the second half of the seventh century, but it is unlikely there were many of them. The conquest happened when the new kingdom of Wessex had just been welded together following the take-over of the Wessex heartlands in Wiltshire and Hampshire by leaders from the Oxfordshire and Berkshire region. Capturing Somerset must have helped to relieve tensions among the newly-amalgamated ruling groups. We know that many Old Welsh warriors continued to live in Wessex – reduced in social status but still functioning as land-holders – and of course the Old Welsh peasantry remained on the land, forming the bulk of the population. What changed over the centuries was that Old Welsh ceased to be the language of the people and was replaced by Old English.

In many respects the Anglo-Saxon newcomers adapted the pattern which they found. Successive kings of Wessex kept much of the land in their direct control, probably taking over great estates which were already functioning before the Anglo-Saxon conquest. Places such as Taunton, Williton, Bruton, Somerton, Frome, Cannington, Carhampton, North and South Petherton, Crewkerne and Cheddar were all Anglo-Saxon royal sites, the *tun* element found in some of the names being suggestive of the importance attaching to these places. Other sites such as Kingsbury Regis (now part of Milborne Port) and Kingsbury Episcopi were probably royal strongholds. Both names contain the elements *cyng* ('king') and *burh* ('strong place or fortification'). The king may have had a hall in each of the Kingsburys – as he certainly did at Cheddar – from which the surrounding areas could be administered. Somerton, 'the summer settlement', was probably the shire's pre-eminent royal centre because of its proximity to the old Roman site at Ilchester and its ability to control the Fosse Way as well as the routes leading east to Wilton and Winchester. Somerton evidently gave its name early on to the *Sumorsæte* ('the dwellers around, or dependent on, Somerton'), and by the Norman Conquest that name was being used to describe the shire itself.

*

The history of Wessex in the seventh and eighth centuries is one of near continuous warfare. Conflict between the English kingdoms was endemic and civil war common. In 722 the queen, Aethelburh, destroyed Taunton, perhaps when a civil war was in progress, and in 733 Aethelbald, king of the Mercians, captured Somerton. Although the armies of the time were tiny (in 786 Cyneheard tried to overthrow King Cynewulf of Wessex with an army of 84 men) the warriors needed to be supported and this was one of the most important duties of a ruler. One way to provide such support was to give the warriors estates of their own, and many parts of the huge royal estates were granted for life for this reason. Other parts of great estates were occupied by groups who owed tribute to the lord at the centre: such were the places called Charlton, a name meaning 'the farmstead of the *ceorls*' (the free peasants of Old English society). And some estates were granted to specialists such as priests (the Prestons) or used to support adult, but not independent, children – probably the king's – giving rise to places called Chilton ('the *tun* of the *cild*').

Very few archaeological remains from this period have been identified and documentary evidence which enables us to reconstruct the daily lives of ordinary people is almost non-existent. It seems that the countryside was farmed by people living in single farmsteads and small hamlets, usually on sites that had been occupied for many centuries: there is growing evidence, for example, that places with *wic* names (giving the modern Wick, Wyke or Week) have direct connections with the Romano-British landscape and may represent sites continuously inhabited since that time. By the year 900 the majority of places recorded by Domesday Book in 1086 were probably already in existence, though here we are talking of estates, not villages. A well-developed network of roads, based upon the old Roman pattern, but using many other routes as well, also existed. Roads were often used as the boundaries of estates described in ninth- and tenth-century land charters, suggesting that the roads pre-date the boundaries. There are twenty-nine cases where boundaries follow roads. At Rimpton, for example, the modern B3184 was the herepath ('military road, through road') of the mid-tenth-century boundary, a road which the parish boundary still follows today.

The Church formed part of the political structure within which the Anglo-Saxon kings governed. We do not know how the Church was organised during the Old Welsh period but after the arrival of the English we see the foundation of monasteries as centres of religious life for the new kingdom. Glastonbury was certainly in being by about 681 when it was given an estate at Pennard, and a year later it received an estate at Creechbarrow close to Taunton, together with woodland on the Quantocks. Muchelney Abbey also existed by the late seventh century when it was granted a large estate by King Ine. Together with the well-known monasteries, the English also founded a number of important minster churches. By the early eighth century the minster of St Andrew already existed at Wells – although the bishop's seat remained at Sherborne until 909 – and the church there probably held extensive estates and was served by a group of priests. Other important churches at Banwell and Congresbury also had religious communities, while the minster church of St Andrew at Northover was sited close to an ancient burial ground for Roman Ilchester, suggesting origins which may long predate the arrival of the English. Elsewhere, important churches were founded at royal centres. Thus, Frome's church of St John the Baptist was founded by St Aldhelm as a monastery, possibly before 700, and

Holy well beneath the Lady Chapel, Glastonbury Abbey, by S.G. Tovey, 1839. The existence of the well may have influenced the siting of the earliest monastic buildings at Glastonbury.

Anglo-Saxon charter of King Aethelred II ('the Unready'), dated AD 995. The charter is a confirmation to Muchelney Abbey that it is the rightful owner of places called Ile Mynister (Ilminster) and Cantmael (West Camel).

The Court House and St Andrew's Church, Congresbury, by J.C. Buckler, 1828. Alfred the Great gave monasteries at Congresbury and Banwell to his servant Asser in about AD 886.

other major churches were founded at places such as Crewkerne, North Petherton, Cannington, Bruton and Taunton. The English pattern of church creation was designed to meet the needs of the new society but incorporated important cult sites from the previous regime.

*

The greatest challenge faced by the Anglo-Saxons was the long campaign of plunder and settlement undertaken by the Danes during the ninth century. The campaign started with a seaborne attack on Carhampton in 843, and reached a

crisis in 878 when 'all the people of Somerset and of Wiltshire and of that part of Hampshire which was on the side of the sea' rallied to King Alfred who then famously defeated the Danes at Edington in Wiltshire. Wessex suffered further attack in the 890s and was saved not least by what had been learnt from developments on the Continent. Stimulated in part by what he had seen in Gaul, Alfred constructed a series of forts or 'burhs' at important points around Wessex. A fort at Lyng, for example, guarded the king's tun at Somerton from possible invasion across the marshes, and was made by driving a ditch across high ground from marsh to marsh. Other sites, such as Axbridge, which protected Cheddar, probably had a square enclosure, a ditch and a bank, while Ilchester and Bath had Roman defences which may have been re-used. Alfred also developed a rating system, called hidation, as a means of ensuring that the forts were maintained and manned after their construction.

The tenth century was a period of expansion, when the population grew and major changes in the organisation of society took place. The towns of Somerset were developed to provide secure centres for the marketing of both local and imported goods. The new kings of the English – as the kings of Wessex had become by the end of the century – needed money, and the expansion of trade made England a money economy which was too big to be organised from the king's hall. Towns provided the setting in which the new specialists, the merchants, could work under the king's control and where the minting of money could take place safely. By the time of Domesday Book in 1086 there were important towns at Bath, Ilchester, Taunton and Milborne Port, but other smaller boroughs also existed at Bruton, Langport, Milverton and Axbridge, while mints at Crewkerne, South Petherton and Watchet and markets at Frome and Ilminster also point to rising economic activity. The most important trade in the late tenth century was with France – with the rising power of Normandy, where Rouen was the greatest trading city, with Brittany, and to a lesser extent with cities such as Nantes, further south. Clearly, Somerset was not well placed to deal directly with such centres, but may have taken advantage of the trade which came from Exeter *en route* for the Midlands via the Fosse Way.

A changing society was reflected not only in the growth of towns. The rural population also began to increase – since nearly all people got their living from the land or depended directly on those who did – and during the tenth and eleventh centuries the rural landscape was transformed. In particular, villages began to appear. There is little evidence that the villages of Somerset existed before the tenth or even the eleventh century. Although places are frequently mentioned in Anglo-Saxon charters it seems that estates rather than villages are

The Alfred Jewel, the most celebrated artefact to have survived from Anglo-Saxon England. It was found at North Petherton in 1693, and has an inscription which reads: + AELFRED MEC HEHT GEWYRCAN ('Alfred ordered me to be made').

Engraving showing Alfred the Great in hiding in the swineherd's hut at Athelney shortly before his victory at the Battle of Edington, AD 878.

The Hanging Chapel and All Saints' Church, Langport, by J.C. Buckler, 1830. The Saxon settlement at Langport was evidently focused on the hill-top site now occupied by the church and chapel.

being referred to. Emerging evidence points to the growth and often the foundation of villages as part of a deliberate reshaping of rural communities, a process most marked in lowland Somerset, east of the Parrett and the Tone. In the western highland areas of the county, where the terrain was less favourable to change, the older pattern of dispersed settlements persisted and still forms the basis of the landscape today. It is improbable that Anglo-Saxon nobility and great churchmen deliberately set out to found villages on their estates and far more likely that what they were doing was reconstructing the agricultural system. They rearranged the fields of each community so that all the land was grouped together into great open fields which could be worked by a community of peasants. The creation of a village was the natural outcome of such re-planning, since the fields now covered many of the ancient farmsteads. It was more efficient for everyone to live close together, near the centre of the estate, and to move out each day into the surrounding fields. This is certainly the picture revealed by field archaeology at Shapwick in central Somerset, and the patterns of planned villages have also been recognised elsewhere.

Silver penny minted at Watchet in the reign of King Cnut by the moneyer Godcild. The coin dates from the period 1017-23.

The new open-field communities were often created at the same time as older, larger, estates were being divided into smaller units. A good example of such a division is provided by the Chinnocks, which seem to have been carved out of a single original estate into East, West and Middle Chinnock, all of which certainly existed by 1066. The division probably took place in the second half of the tenth century. In 1066 East Chinnock belonged to Edmer Ator, a landowner of some importance, while West and Middle Chinnock were held by men too humble to be named who were simply 'thegns'. In the same way, the main settlement at Shapwick was held by the monastery of Glastonbury in 1066, while its subsidiary settlements at Catcott, Edington, Sutton Mallet and Chilton Polden were held by fourteen thegns. Newton St Loe provides another example of village creation. Its name (*niwe tun*, 'the new village') appears in Domesday Book, suggesting that its foundation probably took place in the tenth or eleventh century. Recent work certainly demonstrates that the village existed on the present site in the eleventh century with its fields laid out around it.

The continuing demand for thegns who would serve the king as soldiers in time of need was probably the driving force behind the division of estates. The expansion of the warrior class placed extra burdens on the countryside and the new open field system provided a means of harnessing the labour of the peasants more effectively. Each estate had a demesne farm (the home farm of the lord) which was worked for him mostly by peasants who held their own farmsteads in return for this duty. Such a system could not operate without a large labour force which had to be tied to the land to prevent migration to easier condi-

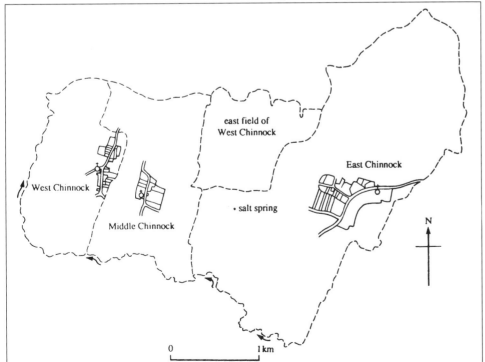

Map of the estate at Chinnock and its pre-Conquest divisions.

tions. The new system was employed most systematically on estates belonging to the monasteries, which were revived and expanded in the tenth century, and it may be that the monks were the men who first introduced open-field agriculture in order to pay for extensive new buildings and for growing monastic communities. In this militarised society the monks were God's warriors and they too needed support.

As the population grew, government became more complex. Before King Alfred's time the king ruled through a system of *ealdormen* – nobles, probably related to the royal family, who governed the shire and commanded its military forces. Thus, in 848 ealdorman Eanwulf of Somerset and ealdorman Osric of Dorset successfully led their combined shire forces against the Danes in a battle at the mouth of the River Parrett. By the middle of the tenth century 'hundreds' had been created: these were groupings of communities which sent representatives to monthly hundred courts held at local meeting-places such as the Bempstone, near Stone Allerton. Cases relating to civil, criminal and religious matters were settled at the hundred courts, while more serious matters, particularly those concerned with the property of thegns and other noble people, and important religious cases, were dealt with in the shire court, presided over by the king's ealdorman and the bishop. Both levels of government were involved in the collection of taxes, and the king's shire reeve acted at each level as the chief administrator and intermediary.

*

The Norman Conquest in 1066 is rightly regarded as the great watershed in English medieval history. Within a few years a ruling aristocracy was swept away and a new group of Norman rulers with new ways of doing things took control. The Normans were a militarised aristocracy, just like the people they displaced, and their success in conquering the countryside inevitably led to changes. As important for us is the fact that the new king, William the Conqueror, ordered the survey we call Domesday Book, which was compiled in 1086. Because of the historical as well as topographical approach adopted in the survey, we have a huge amount of information about England in the second half of the eleventh century, far more than is available for any other European country. Domesday Book shows that Somerset had filled up during the tenth and eleventh centuries. Although inhabitants were not numerous by modern standards – perhaps 65,000 in all – farming activity was very widespread: Domesday reveals a shire in which most of the lowland was extensively ploughed. There was about twice as much woodland as exists now, including the large Forest of Selwood near Bruton, and major wooded areas in the far north-west near Clevedon and along the borders with Dorset and Devon as well as on the slopes of the Quantocks, the Brendons and Exmoor. Most of the central marshlands were still undrained, but all the higher ground was well occupied. Around the Mendips large, wealthy estates with ancient origins still belonged to the Church and the King – places such as Chew Magna, Chewton Mendip, Cheddar, Westbury sub Mendip, Banwell and Winscombe, all of which exploited their favoured positions and possessed ample farm lands together with marshland and moor. In the west the rough moorlands supported fewer people, but such areas were nevertheless well populated. The transfer of land from the English was virtually completed by 1086. About 160 hides of land were still in the hands of Englishmen – about seventy-five of them – so that their holdings were on average very small. The king was the most important secular landowner in the shire, and under him Norman landowners were divided between forty-four tenants-in-chief and their sub-tenants.

The Normans introduced castles into the shire at Montacute, Dunster and Neroche, but by the end of Henry I's reign there were others at Stogursey, Castle Cary and East Harptree. To begin with the purpose of the castles was to control the shire for the Normans, and the successful defence of the new Montacute castle against a local uprising in 1068 showed how important such strongholds could be. As the threat of revolt receded, however, castles became significant to the new aristocracy as bases for furthering their own political ambitions. The

Anglo-Norman aristocracy was used to a system where each family strove to increase its influence by the acquisition of new estates, by marriage and by political alliance, so a castle was a sign of power and social standing as well as being of great practical value. The position of the Anglo-Norman baronage was threatened in the early Norman period by the struggles between the sons of William the Conqueror for control of the Anglo-Norman empire. The rebellions of Odo of Bayeux and the Bishop of Coutances at the beginning of William Rufus's reign, and the disturbances of Henry I's reign, were the result. The powerful Mortain family lost their Somerset possessions because of their support for Duke Robert, the Conqueror's son, who was defeated at the battle of Tinchebrai in 1106. The later struggle for control of the kingdom between King Stephen and the Empress Matilda led to sieges at William FitzJohn's castle at East Harptree and Ralph Lovel's castle at Castle Cary.

One hundred years after Domesday the king's possessions in Somerset had been almost completely alienated, and his relationship with all but the most important landowners had grown increasingly distant. Lesser families, who held their land as tenants of the tenants-in-chief, had emerged as the most important local people on a day-to-day basis. The introduction of primogeniture for inheritance helped families to consolidate their properties and encouraged them to form a long-lasting relationship with the county. Thus, the Hussey family, who held Wilmington, Charlcombe and Batheaston from St Peter's Abbey, Bath, in 1086, were still tenants of the monastery in 1166 and the family continued to hold land by knight service from the abbey in the mid-fourteenth century. Such families were thoroughly anglicised by the time of Henry II, and frequently married the female heirs of Old English landowners. But the growth of more distant relationships between the king and the landowners, and the spread of primogeniture, ensured that those landowners formed a different type of society from that which had existed before the Conquest.

Aerial photograph, 1928, showing the village of Montacute and St Michael's Hill. Robert, Count of Mortain, had established a castle on the hill by 1068 when it was besieged during a revolt against Norman rule.

North-east view of Dunster Castle, by Samuel and Nathaniel Buck, 1733. The hill which rises behind the castle had been fortified by William de Mohun, sheriff of Somerset, by 1086.

The people on whom the landowners relied to support them, the peasant farmers, continued to be as unfree as they had always been, though the practice of slavery, so common in Anglo-Saxon society, seems to have disappeared by 1154. The peasantry included a large number of unfree tenant farmers, each typically holding about a virgate of land. But there were many people with smaller holdings and a growing army of the nearly landless who worked for wages. There were also increasing numbers of small freeholders whose estates may have resulted from the division of property among the very smallest landlords or the sale or grant of small pieces of land by monasteries. The exploitation of the land continued according to the pattern developed in the tenth and eleventh centuries. On the one hand were the very large former royal estates as well as those of the monastic communities. On the other hand were the secular estates, most of which were much smaller, with smaller areas of land and smaller villages as a result. A dichotomy in the size and character of estates which had been the result of the social and economic arrangements of the tenth century was perpetuated in the landscape by the Norman settlement.

Along with a rising population in the countryside went a growth in the number of towns. The old Anglo-Saxon towns had grown in size and new towns developed at places such as Wiveliscombe, Minehead, Dulverton, Milverton, Yeovil, Shepton Mallet and Wells. By the mid-twelfth century there was nowhere suitable left for founding new villages and the expansion of revenues for great landowners was to come from the use of capital to intensify agriculture and from activities such as the draining of marshes. Somerset as we know it had emerged.

LORDS AND TENANTS

2

LORDS AND TENANTS

Mary Siraut

The main preoccupation of rural communities in the Middle Ages was the growing, harvesting and marketing of food, and the continuing struggle to find new land suitable to be farmed. The rapid growth in population after the eleventh century, especially during the middle years of the thirteenth century, placed great pressure on the land and encouraged farmers to exploit every area capable of cultivation. Hill land was reclaimed ('assarted'), wetland was drained for meadow and pasture, and everywhere woodland was cleared, even in the great Royal Forest of Selwood.

As a result, landscapes throughout the county were transformed. By the 1340s a manorial estate with moated manor house and a park of 300 acres had been created from common marshland south of Wincanton. At Sowy island – which comprised Weston Zoyland, Middlezoy and Othery – cultivated land was extended by ditching, so that by 1240 almost a thousand additional acres had been brought into use. It was probably also in this period that individuals and communities began to build earth and stone banks in order to reclaim salt marshes from the sea around the Parrett estuary. At Pawlett, on the east side of the estuary, hay was being made on the Pawlett Hams by the mid-twelfth century. Although high tides, including those which occurred in 1259, could still return the land to the sea, over 350 acres of the south Hams were in agricultural use by the late thirteenth century. Such land was both fertile and valuable, and

The estuary of the River Parrett seen from the Quantock Hills, after a painting by William Hyde.

in the 1330s Stretcholt tithing in Pawlett, which included much new land, was one of the most heavily taxed places in the county. By the end of the Middle Ages even the warths – the salt grasslands which had colonised the silt between the sea defences and the coast or river bank – were being reclaimed for agriculture use.

Land reclamation on the hills was less dramatic, but demand for pasture on the Quantocks, for example, led to the clearance of large areas of furze and heath for grazing, and also to the creation of small enclosures for meadow, as at Ivyton, or for growing oats, as on Buncombe Hill, both in Broomfield parish. Further north, vast tracts of the Quantock ridge belonged to the honors of Stogursey and Nether Stowey, whose lords prevented clearance or enclosure by claiming exclusive rights of common for their tenants against those of smaller local lords.

Mixed farming was typical of most areas in Somerset throughout the Middle Ages, and depended on maintaining a balance between the amount of land plough animals could work and the amount of land required to feed them. Because plough and milch animals could not survive the winter on rough grazing, hay for winter fodder was essential, and hay meadows were correspondingly precious: such land was usually held in common even when open-field arable farming was not practised, and at Shepton Beachamp in 1340 a free tenant, wearing white gloves and carrying a white rod, was required to attend in the common meadow to supervise the mowing and ricking on behalf of all. Where necessary, land was converted to meadow from other uses. At North Wootton in 1189, for example, some pasture was enclosed as meadow land; and in the early fourteenth century at Walton new meadows were created by digging ditches and clearing thorns. A few hill parishes such as Aisholt on the Quantocks made hay in upland pastures known as dry meadows. But where parishes found it impossible to maintain a balance between arable and grass they were usually forced to reduce cultivation and to increase sheep grazing.

Methods of cultivation were never uniform in Somerset. Most communities practised open-field farming in a two- or three-field system, although a few had more fields or had separate systems for each hamlet. Some parishes, especially in West Somerset, probably never possessed open fields at all. In the Brendon parish of Brompton Ralph, for example, closes were in use for growing oats and rye during the fourteenth century. Similarly, at East Quantoxhead, large enclo-

A ploughman and a sower depicted on the chancel screen of All Saints' Church, Norton Fitzwarren, c 1500.

sures cropped in rotation were used for producing wheat early in the fifteenth century; but in about the 1380s at nearby Kilton, wheat was being grown in open fields on a three-year cycle. Diversity of practice was also apparent in South Somerset. The woodland parish of Whitestaunton, for example, was farmed in closes during the Middle Ages, while only a few miles away at Shepton Beauchamp the open fields remained in use as late as the nineteenth century.

*

Although some subsistence freeholders or squatters claimed a degree of independence for themselves by creating homes in remoter areas, most of the rural population was organised into a manorial structure which continued to regulate agricultural practice long after the death of the feudal system. It was the manor court which enforced the local rules, or customs, by which landholding and land management were governed. Such customs were mutual obligations, affecting both lord and tenant, and ensured that buildings, ditches, hedges and droves were kept in repair, that commons were not overstocked, that crops were protected from destruction by livestock and that strays were put in the manor pound. Using the copyhold system – under which tenants were admitted to their properties in open court and given a copy of the court record as proof of title – the manor also imposed agreements concerning land use and good husbandry. In addition, the court appointed reeves, tithingmen, haywards and aletasters, who enforced the day-to-day regulation of agricultural life, and more specialised officials such as the 'wikmen' chosen at Chedzoy in the 1330s, who ensured that the Port and Long walls were kept in repair.

Within the typical Somerset manor the lord's home farm, or demesne, usually covered several hundred acres and was worked by unfree tenants ('villeins') who owed labour services or 'works': about 9,000 works were available to the lord of Stogursey in 1297, but even so, extra labour had to be bought in. The tenants themselves had much smaller holdings. The largest were normally a virgate in extent – about 40 acres – though most tenants held half a virgate or less. Successful tenants sometimes took on a second holding or more commonly would acquire 'overland', newly-cultivated land or former demesne which owed no works and was held for a cash rent. There were also many small freeholders, who might occupy a quarter of the land in some parishes but who remain largely invisible in the surviving records. On the lands of both lord and tenants, barley for malting, oats and rye were all widely grown. But wheat was the chief arable crop in most of the county and was preferred whenever possible. It had a high cash value and most manors aimed to produce a surplus for the market. Oats and rye were grown where the ground was too poor for wheat, and on the Nettlecombe demesne, for example, oats accounted for half the arable produce of the manor in the 1380s and for a quarter of the income, excluding rents. Oats were needed in large quantities when horses were kept and especially on manors where absentee lords and ecclesiastical officials travelled widely. Isabel de Forz, Countess of Devon and Aumale and lady of Crewkerne, moved around her estates with a retinue which consumed two thirds of the oats available from the manor in 1267–8. In addition to the standard crops, mixed grains known as maslin and dredge were also widely grown, as were crops chiefly used for animal feed such as peas, beans and vetches. These last crops were labour intensive and in 1343 at Ashcott forty-two women were employed to plant 6 acres of beans.

Other crops exploited in the Middle Ages included fruit, garden vegetables, timber and seaweed. Most manors had orchards to provide apples and pears for the table and some produced cider. Vegetables such as leeks and onions are recorded, and the tenants of Steart near Stogursey owed garlic rents in the thirteenth century. Woodland management was universally practised producing timber, coppice wood and underwood for building, hurdles, furniture, tools and fuel. Timber from royal forests and parks was often granted for building. North Petherton Park, for example, supplied timber for Bridgwater and Stogursey castles, Glastonbury and Cleeve abbeys and Somerton gaol; it also supplied fuel wood to Buckland Priory at East Lyng until the Dissolution. Glastonbury had its

Early thirteenth century capital in the south transept of Wells Cathedral depicting a vineyard robber (or apple stealer) and his accomplice.

The West Somerset coast at Shurton Bars, Stogursey. Seaweed, or 'ore', was gathered here in the Middle Ages for burning as fertiliser, and later for glass-making.

firewood brought from Baltonsborough by the tenants of several manors and peat was stacked by them at the abbot's manor house in Meare. Seaweed was collected along the Somerset coast in the form of laver for consumption and of ore for burning as fertiliser and later for glass making. Licences to burn ore were granted at Stogursey in the fifteenth century, and at East Quantoxhead the lord stipulated that the smoke from burning should not reach the manor house.

Livestock was a vital part of the mixed farming system and most manorial lords employed drovers, oxherds, shepherds and swineherds. The oxen which served as the usual plough and cart beasts, and the mares used as draught animals on some Somerset manors, were of course highly prized. But livestock of many other kinds could be found in plenty. Some larger landowners, for example, had specialist dairies. The Glastonbury Abbey dairy at Baltonsborough had about 40 cows in the late thirteenth century, producing over 300 cheeses and 12 stone of butter, and also herds of goats and pigs. Production reached a peak of 406 cheeses and 16 stone of butter in 1304 when a second cowshed was built with a roof requiring 75 tiles. The dairy at East Quantoxhead comprised 11 cows in 1405, but by 1415 the milk of five of them was sold, as was also commonly the practice on Glastonbury manors in the later Middle Ages. At Crewkerne – an estate with 64 nanny goats in 1086 – cheese was produced from sheep in the late thirteenth century and two women were employed for seventeen weeks to milk ewes.

Sales of wool made large sheep flocks profitable and landowners with several manors could move flocks around, as happened regularly on the Glastonbury estates. The abbey's manor at Walton proved a particularly unlucky place for the flock: in 1344 the wool was stolen from 14 ewes, and 142 lambs were brought from Glastonbury in 1354 to replace a flock which had died. Regular outbreaks of disease occurred in the fifteenth century, especially in 1428 when 367 sheep died. The abbey's herd of goats was moved from Baltonsborough after an outbreak of disease, and in 1304 they were installed in a new house at Godney before being moved in 1313 to Meare where 41 kids were born. The abbey tenants at Baltonsborough kept their own goats as well, 256 of which got into the lord's woods in 1304. Pigs, like poultry, were kept on even the smallest holdings and were often allowed to roam free, although most manors insisted that pigs were ringed and that a payment for 'pannage', generally 1d per animal, was made to the lord to allow pigs to forage in his woodland.

Given such large quantities of livestock, grazing was a constant source of disputes. Commons were 'driven', 'chased' or 'preyed' annually and animals found grazing illegally were shut in the pound. It was not only the lowly whose animals were impounded, or who found themselves involved in disputes about

Glastonbury Abbey and the abbey precinct, after a drawing by William Stukeley, 1723. The abbots of Glastonbury were Somerset's most powerful ecclesiastical landlords throughout the Middle Ages.

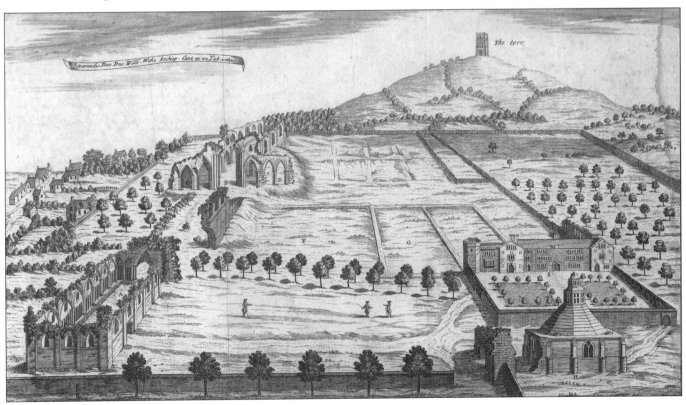

Barn belonging to Glastonbury Abbey on its estate at Pilton, by W.W. Wheatley, 1846. Other barns which belonged to the abbey survive at Doulting and at Glastonbury itself.

grazing. In 1332 the prior of Stogursey complained that his horse, a colt, 18 oxen, 200 sheep and lambs, a boar and 30 pigs had been illegally impounded by his neighbour Robert FitzPayn. The Bishop of Bath and Wells had his piggery on the levels destroyed by the Abbot of Glastonbury's men in the 1270s, and despite an agreement that the pigs should not be disturbed, the piggery was broken down again in 1315. Agreements for the fair division of the moors were always short-lived and in 1299 the men of the Dean of Wells were beaten up by those of the abbot in a dispute over trees on the moors. As well as grazing and firewood, the levels provided reed for thatching, peat and fish, all of which were the subject of further acrimony between bishop and abbot and between abbot and dean.

Although much of the produce of the countryside was consumed locally, there was also a substantial market in produce the mechanics of which are not always clear. Tenants on the Bishop of Winchester's manor of Rimpton owed carrying services to markets at Ilchester, Yeovil, Sherborne and Castle Cary, while those at Holway near Taunton could be required to take grain to Topsham in Devon and to load it on ships. Most of the regular markets were held in towns, but there were also rural markets such as that at Shepton Beauchamp which had its own shambles in the fifteenth century. More important, especially for livestock, were the great rural fairs. Lopen fair was in existence by 1201 and was held by the Crown from the late thirteenth century. It lasted for seven days at Whitsuntide but declined after the establishment of White Down fair in 1361. White Down, at the junction of several routes near Cricket St Thomas, was one of Somerset's most important fairs. Another was Priddy, said to have moved out of Wells in 1348 to avoid the plague.

*

The privileges of wealth and power possessed in varying degrees by manorial lords were expressed in many ways. Landlords could command from their tenants, or obtain from their demesnes, food of a kind rarely tasted by those who produced it. Squabs from the dovecote, honey from the skep, fish from the mere, eggs offered at Easter, capon and spice rents and the best beast from the goods of the recently-deceased ensured that the lord ate well whatever the season. In the 1490s St Augustine's Abbey, Bristol, received annually from its tenants at Pawlett 300 hens eggs and 200 stone of cheese, as well as cattle, young pigs and geese. Deer, rabbits and doves were the preserve of the landowner despite the depredations of such animals on the crops of tenant farmers. Deer parks, incorporating deer leaps, were established by many private landowners and maintained as wooded pasture. In 1229 the Bishop of Bath was allowed to disafforest North

Circular dovecote belonging to Dunster Priory, by S.G. Tovey, 1846. Bath Priory was granted an estate at Dunster in about 1100, and had soon established a small monastic community there. It survived until 1539.

West view of Stogursey Castle, by Samuel and Nathaniel Buck, 1733. The castle was probably built by William de Curci (d. c 1114) and was the seat of the honor or barony of Stogursey. It was refortified in 1233 but fell into decay during the sixteenth century.

The abbot of Glastonbury's fish house, Meare, by J.C. Buckler, 1828. The adjoining Meare Pool had been drained by the mid-eighteenth century.

Curry to make a park and when Richard Musgrove created a park near Brewham he received a grant of royal deer to stock it. The owner of Yarlington manor was not content with the hundred-acre deer park next to his manor house and in the early fourteenth century cleared a wood on the other side of the parish to create another. Although park pasture could be let out, parks were nevertheless expensive to maintain: Glastonbury Abbey required the tenants of most of its manors to contribute to the upkeep of the park at Pilton during the Middle Ages. Many landowners also had rabbit warrens or coneygars. The Beauchamp family had a warren at Ham Hill in 1339, the year in which a thousand rabbits were stolen from it, and by the sixteenth century Stogursey Castle was among the more unusual of numerous rabbit warrens recorded in the county.

Fisheries, like parks, dovecotes and coneygars, usually belonged to the lord and could be of considerable extent. At Meare, where both the mere and river weirs were productive, the tenants of the Abbot of Glastonbury were responsible

for the fishing and for carrying fish to the abbey every day during Lent. Four boats were kept on the mere in the early fourteenth century, when the water produced large quantities of eels, pike and bream and also provided a home for the abbot's swans. But the fishery declined from the mid-fourteenth century as the lake silted up and reed beds reduced its size. By the early sixteenth century the fishery was regarded as being no more than a place of recreation for the abbot and monks. Sea fisheries in the form of weirs were usually held of the Crown, but at Stolford they belonged to Stogursey Priory. Illegal salmon weirs were sometimes built across river mouths, as at Doniford in the fourteenth century, and thus prevented the fish from spawning.

The mills which were so prominent a feature in the landscape of medieval Somerset were also in many cases the property of manorial lords, who tried to exercise a monopoly in grinding the corn of tenant farmers. Throughout much of the county watermills predominated as they were cheaper to maintain and easier to operate; but windmills were common in the levels, where water flows were inadequate, and on the hills of central Somerset. Though most mills ground corn, others were adapted for fulling cloth and later for grinding edge tools. Few can have been as substantial as Bow Mill, Martock, which had a great gate, extensive domestic quarters, a bakehouse, a furnace, a dovecote, stables and a wagon house. Walton windmill was built in 1342 to serve as a customary mill for Walton and Street manors, but it was not popular and large numbers of tenants were presented at the manor court for not using it. At Chedzoy the early watermill was replaced by windmills in the early fourteenth century. One blew down in 1379 but was immediately rebuilt and another was bought second-hand at Barrington, dismantled and brought to Chedzoy where it was re-erected in the East Field. There it remained, no doubt with later alterations and improvements, in the centre of the great open wheat field which was the scene of the bloody aftermath of the Battle of Sedgemoor, until it was blown down and destroyed by a great storm in 1827.

Piles Mill, Selworthy, c 1910. The mill evidently dates from the sixteenth century, with later alterations.

Windmill and miller depicted on an early sixteenth century bench end in St Mary's Church, Bishop's Lydeard, by W.W. Wheatley, 1848.

The refectory, Cleeve Abbey, in use as a farm building, by S.G. Tovey, 1845. The refectory, which Pevsner calls 'one of the finest rooms in Somerset', was built by William Dovel, the last abbot (1507–37).

Some changes to the landscape were of a kind that only especially powerful lords could achieve. Glastonbury Abbey drove large-scale drainage schemes through the levels, changing the course of rivers such as the Brue. Athelney Abbey built the Baltmoor wall in the mid-twelfth century to divert the West Yeo, a branch of the Tone, and made subsequent alterations to the Tone in agreement with the Dean and Chapter of Wells. And in 1280 Glastonbury enclosed Aller moor with the Great Wall despite attempts by Ralph of Aller to bribe the abbey steward with a 'noble cockerel'. Lesser lords also undertook improvement schemes, though on a more modest scale. At Williton, for example, man-made watercourses were built in the fourteenth century to divert local streams into the meadows, and similar waterleats were also created on the neighbouring manors of Doniford and Nettlecombe.

*

The first half of the fourteenth century saw a decline in agricultural productivity, owing at least in part to bad weather and disease. Deterioration in the climate may have led to poorer grain yields and to the disappearance of vineyards such as those at Meare, cleared for orchard and pasture by 1344. Poor harvests in turn weakened the increasingly numerous labouring population and probably made it impossible for many farmers to pay rents and other dues. At Widcombe, near Martock, for example, it was said that an unfair tax assessment had caused the depopulation of the tithing, all the inhabitants having left except for five poor men and various sub-tenants, none of whom were liable to pay. The Black Death of 1348, traditionally regarded as the cause of agricultural crisis in the fourteenth century, was in reality probably only the last straw. Its immediate effects were certainly catastrophic, and many parishes suffered devastating mortality. At Crowcombe the rental fell from £8 13s 4d in 1342 to 5s in 1349 because the tenants were dead of the plague, though there is evidence of recovery by 1352; at Poundisford, near Taunton, more than fifty holdings were vacant in 1349; at Chedzoy sixteen tenants died in 1348 and although new tenants were immediately admitted to vacant holdings, further deaths lead to several holdings remaining in the lord's hands; at North Cadbury many tenants died; and at South Cadbury it was said that there were no surviving tenants at all.

The Black Death, and recurrences of plague later in the century, greatly reduced the population and led to the abandonment of often marginal land improved for cultivation in the twelfth and thirteenth centuries. At the same time the lord's hold over his tenants was weakening. In 1360 eighteen men and women refused to do outdoor work on Chedzoy manor and withdrew their labour. At Street in 1366 most works had been released or lost and part of the demesne had been fallow for three years. Manumissions (grants of freedom to villein tenants) became common from the fourteenth century onwards, although as late as the sixteenth century a few unfree tenants remained on some manors including Chedzoy, Kilton and a few of the Glastonbury estates. On other manors, such as Nettlecombe, all services had been commuted before the end of the fifteenth century. Labour became expensive, despite government attempts to fix wages, and for landlords the costs of agricultural production rose. The widespread abandonment of demesne farming was one of the results. After the death in 1398 of the lady of Lopen manor, for example, the demesne was divided up and rented out, the new tenant of 23 acres of demesne being required to build a house with a three-bay hall as well as a barn.

By the fifteenth century many manorial landlords derived their entire income from rents; but even rent income was threatened by the frequent unwillingness of tenants to take anything but the best land. At Yeovilton three 60-acre farms were let at reduced rents 'until better tenants should come'. At Chadmead in North Petherton in the 1470s land in hand accounted for over half the estate, though these lands were sold for temporary herbage. In 1474 one enterprising tenant took all the in-hand lands at a reduced rent, pulled down the old cottages and built a single large house on his new farm. Such tenants were also responsible for the piecemeal inclosure of arable which took place in many parishes at this period. On Glastonbury manors such as Walton and Street, arrears of rent were regularly written off, but by the 1470s there was evidence of recovery as new houses and farm buildings were built both for the tenants and for the demesne farm. The dissolution of the monasteries in the 1530s further affected patterns of landholding, leading to the break-up of many former monastic estates and often to the emergence of large leasehold or freehold farms created by new absentee landlords. Many of these landlords were London-based 'asset strippers' such as Sir Edward Peckham, who sold the best holdings at Butleigh, a former Glastonbury estate, on 299-year leases before disposing of what remained.

*

There is something comfortingly familiar about the Somerset countryside at the end of the Middle Ages. The county was well populated; its towns, villages and hamlets were securely established; its churches and manor houses had been built to withstand the passing of time even if its castles were already decaying. Although a few areas of land remained to be tamed, the patchwork of enclosed fields was already beginning to spread from upland parishes into lowland open-field areas. Great social and economic changes lay ahead, but the county of Somerset, as it entered the modern era, was quickly assuming the appearance it would retain for the next 400 years.

SOMERSET PARISH CHURCHES & PARISHIONERS DURING THE MIDDLE AGES

3

SOMERSET PARISH CHURCHES AND PARISHIONERS DURING THE MIDDLE AGES

Joseph Bettey

Few counties can rival Somerset for the number, splendour and interest of its medieval churches. They remain a remarkable tribute to the enduring appeal of the Christian message for Somerset people, and make clear to even the casual observer that the Middle Ages were above all an age of faith. Churches in the county range from simple early buildings, such as Culbone, Swell, Stawley and Sutton Bingham, to the architectural splendours of Wells Cathedral and the extravagant grandeur of Crewkerne, Mells, Axbridge, St Cuthbert's in Wells, St John's in Glastonbury, and St Mary Redcliffe. These medieval buildings, whether austere churches built to serve scattered rural communities or the lavishly-decorated structures of wealthier places, have been hallowed by centuries of prayer and worship, by countless baptisms, marriages and funerals, and by innumerable private petitions and public thanksgivings. They can all reveal much about the fortunes of the successive generations they have served.

Culbone church, photographed in June 1906 during a visit by the Somerset Archaeological and Natural History Society. The church is reputedly the smallest parish church in England.

Wells Cathedral, after a drawing by T.L. Walker, 1837. The present building was begun c 1180. The west front, exclusive of the towers, was completed c 1230–1250.

The building, furnishing and maintenance of medieval churches imposed a heavy burden on local communities, in addition to the demands made on the Somerset economy by the cathedral in Wells and by the county's numerous monasteries and religious houses. Though the Christian Church in the Middle Ages was a centralised, international institution, it was on their own parish churches that most people's pride and affection were focused. The parish church was involved in every stage of life, from baptism and marriage to extreme unction, absolution and burial. Its services and ceremonies gave meaning to an existence which was often both harsh and brief; it was at the heart of the social, educational, charitable and cultural life of the community; and the annual cycle of fasting and festivals, saints' days, holidays and rituals provided the pattern for daily life and marked the passage of each year.

As well as its exceptional legacy of medieval architecture, Somerset is also rich in documentary sources from the later Middle Ages. Surviving records provide evidence of the central role of the church in parish life and of the ways in which money was raised for building work and for providing rich furnishings and decoration. A few Somerset parishes such as Wellow, Farleigh Hungerford, North Cadbury, High Ham and St Mary Redcliffe received large contributions for their churches from wealthy benefactors. But most parishes lacked such advantages, and one striking fact which emerges from late-medieval parish documents is how often the rebuilding, enlargement or decoration of a church depended on the generosity of parishioners alone. The motives of individual donors no doubt ranged from piety and simple enthusiasm for a particular project, through local rivalry with neighbouring parishes over the size of their churches or the height and magnificence of their towers, to concern for personal salvation and fear of the torments of hell so realistically displayed in wall-paintings. But whatever their motives, the result was that remarkable sums of money were raised even from thinly-populated parishes.

From the fifteenth century more than twenty Somerset parishes have sets of churchwardens' accounts, giving details of fund-raising and expenditure. One example comes from St Mary's, Yatton, where accounts survive from 1445. They reveal an amazingly active church life and remarkable fund-raising to finance the

St Mary's Church, Yatton, by G. Hawkins, c 1840. The church is seen as lavishly rebuilt during the fifteenth century.

rebuilding, furnishing and decoration of the church. Money came from gifts, bequests, collections, the hire of the church house, fees for burials and, above all, from church ales. Each year at Whitsun the churchwardens brewed ale, solicited gifts of food and organised plays, games and other activities. Such festivities brought in surprisingly large sums from the parishioners, few of whom were even moderately wealthy. The results of their generosity are still apparent, for during the fifteenth century St Mary's Church was remodelled on the grandest scale. The fact that much of its fine architecture was paid for by impoverished parishioners is remarkable enough, but in addition the accounts reveal that local people also equipped the church with elaborately-carved wooden screens, statues, wall-paintings, pews, vestments, bells, organs and plate, most of which were to be destroyed during the Reformation.

Similar enthusiasm for parish churches is reflected in other late-medieval churchwardens' accounts. At Yeovil the parishioners were encouraged to contribute to church funds through church ales, fees for the use of the bells and the processional cross during funerals, the hire of weights and measures from the church and gifts to the holy taper or candle which was kept burning in the church during Holy Week when parishioners made their confessions. Other income was received from traders whose carts stood along the churchyard wall on market days, and large sums also came from the renting of seats or pews in the church: these were carefully graded so that those occupying the front seats paid the most. Just as profitable were the annual festivities involving Robin Hood, Little John and their companions who used various boisterous methods to extract contributions from parishioners and travellers. In 1519, for example, the churchwardens' accounts include the item:

> Received of Richard Hacker this yere being Robyn
> Hood that by hys gud perswysyon and dylygent labors
> and by the gud devocion of the towne and contrey
> he presentyd to God and Holy Church   £7 0s 7^1/$_2$d

At several other parishes, including Croscombe, Keynsham, Whitchurch, Trull, Banwell and Brent Knoll, groups of young men and women known as 'hoglers' or 'hogglers' were given unofficial licence to collect money for their churches by all sorts of unorthodox tricks and antics as well as by dancing and singing. But everywhere the most lucrative and regular source of income was the church ale. At Trull, for example, the annual midsummer ale consistently produced more than £3. A reminder of the former importance of church ales

The church house, Chew Magna, by J.C. Buckler, 1834.

survives in the church houses often built near parish churches where brewing equipment could be stored and where ales and parish meetings could be held. Examples survive at Crowcombe, Chew Magna, Croscombe, Yatton, Stoke sub Hamdon and Long Ashton. Churchwardens went to considerable trouble to provide entertainment and spectacles that would attract people to the ales. The fine vestments, banners and cross from Yeovil were regularly hired out to neighbouring parishes for their ales; players' costumes could be hired from Sherborne, and there are references to plays, players and costumes from Montacute, Tintinhull and St Michael's in Bath. At Yatton minstrels were regularly engaged.

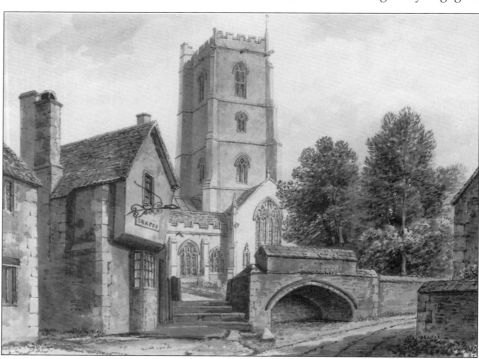

St George's Church, Dunster, by J. Buckler, 1839.

Cornhill and St Mary's Church, Bridgwater, by J.C. Buckler, 1832.

The ultimate responsibility for fund-raising and for all other parish activities rested with the churchwardens. Most parishes had two churchwardens, elected annually and unpaid. They managed the finances, provided materials for the services, employed architects, builders, carpenters, carvers and painters, and purchased the necessary materials for repairs, extensions, furnishings and decoration. The function of the clergy was to conduct the services, and they seldom appear in the accounts, unless they are paid for additional services or are employed to write the accounts for illiterate churchwardens. When the congregation at Dunster decided to rebuild their church tower in 1442, it was the churchwardens who entered into a contract with a local builder, John Marys of Stogursey, and agreed all the details with him. Likewise during the 1490s, when the parishioners of Dunster were in dispute with the monks from Bath abbey, who had a subsidiary cell at Dunster and used part of the church, it was the churchwardens who handled the business and pursued the matter to the Court of Star Chamber in London. At Bridgwater in 1367 it was the churchwardens who made a contract with the Bristol architect, Nicholas Waleys, possibly for building the spire on their church, and throughout Somerset it was the churchwardens who arranged for the installation of pews with the elaborately-carved bench-ends which are such a notable feature of the county's churches. At Yatton during the 1440s the churchwardens organised the construction of a magnificent rood screen, dividing the nave from the chancel. They paid the expenses of men who went to Bristol and Easton in Gordano to inspect screens and to get ideas, no doubt with a view to having an even grander screen at Yatton. They purchased the oak timber and engaged a local craftsman, John Crosse, to work for several years on the project. Finally, they arranged the installation and painting of the screen, and bought 69 statues to stand along it. At various times during the sixteenth century the churchwardens at Trull arranged for the carving of a new rood loft and for other woodwork, including the interesting series of bench-ends which remains in the church today.

Interior of All Saints' Church, Trull, by S.G. Tovey, 1846. The church contains some of the best woodwork to be found in the West Country.

Churchwardens' accounts also describe the profusion of colourful possessions to be found within late-medieval churches. An inventory of 1447 listing goods belonging to St Mary's, Bridgwater, includes silver crosses, candlesticks, censers, chalices, numerous finely-embroidered sets of vestments in blue, green, white and gilt, hangings for the altars and several manuscript service books which were no doubt beautifully illuminated. In 1508 an inventory made by the churchwardens of Pilton includes silver crosses, chalices and ornaments, no fewer than sixteen separate sets of vestments, banners to be carried in processions, and many service books both manuscript and printed. The Pilton accounts reveal that the church was decorated with wall-paintings of the saints, and possessed more than thirty statues, as well as lights, candlesticks, a peal of bells, and a painted rood screen.

*

The late-medieval records leave no doubt of the vitality of parish life and the willingness of parishioners to contribute to their churches. They tell us little, however, about the beliefs and opinions of parishioners, and it is even more difficult to obtain any idea of belief during earlier centuries. One clue may be found in the changing styles and subject matter of the carvings which decorate so many Somerset churches. Carvings from the eleventh and twelfth centuries reveal an emphasis on conflict, on the struggle between the forces of good and evil. This

The north doorway of All Saints' Church, Lullington, by W.W. Wheatley, 1843.

seems to mirror the predominant Christian teaching of the period. Thus, intertwined snakes and dragons fight on the fragment of a ninth-century cross-shaft from West Camel, while capitals in the Saxon church at Milborne Port show griffins attacking a horned figure, presumably representing the devil. On the twelfth-century tympanum above the doorway at Stoke sub Hamdon, Sagittarius fires his arrow at Leo, the lion-like symbol of evil. The corbel table beneath the roof at Stoke is filled with a remarkable collection of weird and hideous creatures, while a small window at the north-west corner of the church has above it a sophisticated carving of St Michael in close conflict with a beautifully-carved dragon. Around the twelfth-century font at Lullington sinister creatures including the horned god lie in wait for the human soul, burdened with original sin. They are only to be overcome through the sacrament of baptism, a fact which the inscription around the bowl of the font makes abundantly clear: *Hoc Fontis Sacro Pereunt Delicta Lavacro* ('through the sacred washing in this font are sins cleansed'). The magnificent figure of Christ sits serene above the north door at Lullington with hand raised in blessing, while all around are the monsters, demons and grotesque creatures which only the power of the Risen Lord can subdue. Clasping the font at Locking are four figures with outstretched arms to protect the child as it is brought to baptism, repelling evil in the form of writhing snakes which threaten the human soul. At East Pennard four sphinxes support the font and crush four devil's heads in the process. A dragon is ready to pounce above the Norman doorway at Flax Bourton, and numerous monsters lurk in the capitals at Stogursey.

Early sixteenth-century bench ends in St Michael's Church, Brent Knoll, by W.W. Wheatley, 1843. A fox, at first depicted wearing a mitre, is put in the stocks and finally hanged by geese. The benches may be a satire on the abbot of Glastonbury, or on Bishop Richard Fox.

Subjects such as these reveal the Church's teaching concerning the struggle against evil, the certainty of judgement and the hope of redemption. They also give a unique insight into the thoughts and hopes of an unlettered congregation. Some carvings illustrate rustic humour, such as the gargoyle in the form of upturned buttocks on the tower at Churchstanton, the man on a privy and holding his nose on the tower vaulting at St Mary Redcliffe, the elephant and rhinoceros on the tower at Camerton, the monkey-musician on the parapet at Crowcombe, or the satirical use of the well-known Reynard the Fox legend on the bench-ends at Brent Knoll. Other carvings present a warning against sexual promiscuity, such as the hideously-ugly and sexually-explicit female figures (known as Sheila-na-Gig) at Stoke sub Hamdon, Fiddington and Clevedon. Warnings against idle gossip or lies are contained in the bench-end at North Cadbury of two gossiping women, and in the 'Tutivillus' bench-end at Charlton Mackrell which shows the demon who collected in his sack fragments of unchar-itable gossip, then carried them off to Hell where they were stored till the Day of Judgement. Most common of all is the figure of the Green Man who retained his popularity with carvers throughout the Middle Ages and appears on corbels and capitals, bench-ends and screens in churches throughout Somerset. Argument continues about whether he is a pagan fertility figure or illustrates natural spring-time regeneration as a symbol of rebirth through Christ.

From the later Middle Ages far more carvings survive, both in stone and wood, but generally the subject matter is quite different. In place of the incessant conflict between good and evil, the emphasis is on the saints, especially the Blessed Virgin, and on the need for intercession in order to attain personal salva-tion or to avoid the pains of purgatory. A whole gallery of medieval saints remains in the niches around the tower at Ile Abbots; the Virgin and Christ Child are on the tower at East Brent, the Virgin's feet resting on the Green Man. Carvings of the Risen Christ are found on the towers at Chewton Mendip and Batcombe; the Holy Trinity appears on the western apex of the nave roof at Yatton; and the figure of the Virgin is carved on the tower at Banwell, together with her emblem of a lily. Among the numerous saints or their emblems which appear on bench-ends, in wall-paintings or in stained glass are St Margaret complete with her dragon at North Cadbury, St John the Baptist at Brent Knoll and Alford, St Christopher at Ditcheat, Wedmore and Cameley, St George at Farleigh Hungerford and Nunney, St Anthony at Winscombe, St Peter at St Catherine's, and St Michael, St Margaret and St George at Trull. The Seven Sacraments are carved on the font at Nettlecombe, while the Crowcombe font has St Anne teaching the Virgin to read. These and other saints were regarded as essential intercessors before the throne of heaven.

It was this desire for the intercession of the Virgin and the saints, and the passionate desire to escape the torments of purgatory, which led to the establishment of so many chantries, both by individuals and by groups or fraternities. For example, there were several religious fraternities at Croscombe, one of which, the guild of St George, was rich enough to spend more than £27 11s 8d on a large statue of St George which was purchased from a carver in Exeter described as a 'Gorge-maker'. Desire for the prayers of subsequent generations also produced the large, late-medieval funeral monuments such as those to the Rodneys at Rodney Stoke, the Wadhams at Ilminster, the St Loes at Chew Magna and the Chokes at Long Ashton.

*

Few people questioned the basic tenets of Christian belief, but some were unwilling to accept all the teachings of the contemporary church. John Wycliffe, the originator of the so-called 'Lollard' heresy, had died in 1384, but a few of his followers were to be found in Somerset throughout the fifteenth and early sixteenth centuries. The bishops' registers record the occasional arrest and trial of heretics, especially of people from the industrial suburbs of Bristol south of the River Avon, in St Thomas's, Temple, St Mary Redcliffe and Bedminster parishes, which were within the Somerset diocese of Bath and Wells. In 1448, for example, Bishop Thomas Bekynton examined John Yonge, the chaplain of the Temple Church, Bristol, on charges that he had denied the authority of the Pope, the necessity of fasting, the confession of sins, pilgrimages, images and prayers to the saints. Yonge was declared a heretic and excommunicated, but since he was old and blind the bishop charitably entrusted him to the custody of the monks at Muchelney. In 1460 Thomas Cole and Agnes his wife, from Norton St Philip, appeared before the bishop's court charged with various heresies, including doubting the value of pilgrimages to the shrine of the Holy Trinity in Bath, the worship of images – Cole and his wife made the mysterious claim that St Peter was 'a dawber of walls' – and in other ways misleading 'wel disposed Cristen people'. They were sentenced to do public penance in Wells and Norton St Philip and solemnly to renounce their heretical beliefs. Other unfortunate people with similar doubts found themselves before the bishop's court during the next few decades, and early in the sixteenth century there are references to the trials of dyers, weavers, smiths, carpenters, a carpet-maker, a wire-drawer and a bow-maker from St Thomas and St Mary Redcliffe, Bristol, on charges of heresy and of holding Lollard beliefs.

Despite the doctrinal doubts of a few people, however, the massive extent of late-medieval building work on Somerset churches in the decades before the

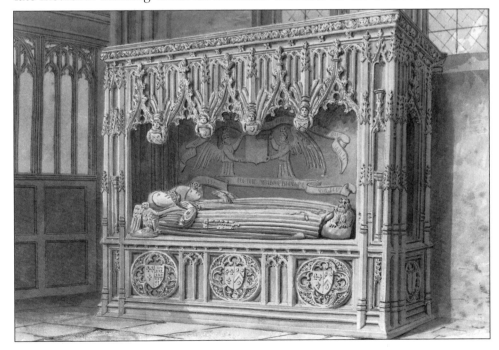

Late-medieval monument at Long Ashton to Sir Richard Choke (d. 1483), a judge of the Court of Common Pleas, and his wife, by J. Buckler, 1829.

Church of St Mary Magdalene, Chewton Mendip, by J. Buckler, 1827. Some regard the tower as Somerset's finest. It was still unfinished as late as 1541.

Reliquary supposed to have contained the blood of St Thomas à Becket. The reliquary was found in Kewstoke church, but may originally have belonged to Woodspring Priory, which was dedicated to the saint.

Reformation shows the continuing strength of support for the churches. In particular, many of Somerset's fine church towers were still being built during the early sixteenth century. The evidence of wills shows that money was left in this period to complete the towers at Chewton Mendip, Batcombe, Mells and Leigh on Mendip; bequests from Taunton merchants for the tower of St Mary's included money, cloth, iron, wine and woad. Such enthusiastic support for church building came to an abrupt halt with the changes of the Reformation, beginning when Henry VIII took the title of Supreme Head of the Church in 1534.

*

Whatever view we take of the Reformation, either as an act of State inspired by royal matrimonial difficulties or as a rejection of late-medieval religious attitudes, there can be no doubt of the wholesale destruction of things of great beauty which resulted. The survival in Somerset of many churchwardens' accounts for the Reformation years provides a detailed picture of the recurrent waves of destruction. At Yatton we can follow the way in which the screens, wall-paintings, bench-ends and windows, which had so recently been provided, were ruthlessly ripped out in adherence to the orders of successive governments. At St Michael's, Bath, during the reign of Edward VI (1547–53), statues of the saints were removed, the entire church was whitewashed with lime to obliterate wall-paintings, and stone altars were dug out to be replaced by a wooden table board. Here as elsewhere, each successive twist and turn of official policy was followed immediately by the churchwardens who were forced into compliance by the powerful apparatus of Tudor government. Everywhere the expense of destruction was trivial compared to the money which had been spent on the profusion of statues, screens, stained glass, plate and service books. At no time, however, do we get any indication in the churchwardens' accounts of their feelings about the bewilderingly rapid changes they were required to make. It is a remarkable feature of English church history that there was no sustained opposition, or outspoken protest, against the destruction of so many treasures. Not even during the reign of Queen Mary (1553–58), when Catholicism was temporarily restored, and churchwardens were required to purchase at great

Carved stones, evidently ranging in date from the twelfth to the sixteenth century, found during excavations at Muchelney Abbey, 1873–4. The abbey was dissolved in 1538 and the abbey church was then progressively destroyed.

St Mary's Church, Yatton, looking west, by J. Buckler, 1829. The bare interior of the church reflects the destruction of its late-medieval furnishings during the Reformation.

expense many of the items they had so recently destroyed or dispersed, is there evidence of the attitudes of the churchwardens. At Yatton, for example, they were obliged to spend £2 17s 4d merely to replace the service books, lamps and censers they had destroyed. The restoration was short-lived, and with the accession of Elizabeth in 1558 further change was ordered. A Book of Common Prayer cost the churchwardens 5s in 1559 and 6d was spent 'in expenses at the plucking down of the images'. The saddest of all the entries made by the Yatton churchwardens recorded 5d spent on demolishing the beautifully-carved rood screen which had been constructed with such care and at such expense a century earlier. With the screens, statues, paintings and stained glass swept away, and all the colours, lights and symbolism removed, it was clear that a new Protestant church had finally emerged with a quite different ethos and a totally changed appeal.

1. *View from near Wells towards Glastonbury Tor, by W.W. Wheatley, c 1840.   Watercolour.*

2. *Church of St Aldhelm, Doulting, signed 'DMG', c 1880. Watercolour. St Aldhelm, the apostle of east Somerset, died at Doulting in AD 709.*

3. *View over Nailsea Moor towards Worlebury and the Bristol Channel, with Cadbury Camp (Tickenham) on the right, by Samuel Jackson, c 1822. Watercolour.*

4. *Cadbury Camp, Tickenham, by Samuel Jackson, c 1822. Watercolour.*

5. *Ruins of Glastonbury Abbey, by S.G. Tovey, c 1840. Watercolour.*

6. *Peat heath, Meare, with Glastonbury Tor in the distance, by W.W. Wheatley, 1844. Watercolour.*

7. *Woodspring Priory, Kewstoke, by Samuel Jackson, 1822. Watercolour.*

8. *Walton Old Church, Walton in Gordano, by Samuel Jackson, 1822. Watercolour.*

9. *Walton Old Church, castle and farm, by Samuel Jackson, 1822. Watercolour.*

10. *St Mary's Church, Kilve, and Kilve 'abbey', by W.W. Wheatley, 1847. Watercolour and bodycolour. The abbey was originally the manor house, and later the residence of a college of priests.*

11. *'Clipping' the church, Shrove Tuesday night, St Lawrence's Church, Rode, by W.W. Wheatley, 1848. Watercolour. The custom illustrated here, once widely observed, was accompanied by shouting intended to frighten away the devil.*

12. *The Wyndham Chapel, St Decuman's Church, Watchet, by S.G. Tovey, c 1840. On the right is the monument to Sir John Wyndham (d. 1574), now partly destroyed, and on the left the monument to Sir William Wyndham (d. 1683).*

13. *View of the ford over Wellow Brook, with the bridge and St Julian's Church, Wellow, by W.W. Wheatley, 1842. Watercolour.*

14. *Church of All Saints, Stockland Bristol, by W.W. Wheatley, c 1840. Watercolour. The church was entirely rebuilt, 1865–6.*

SOMERSET TOWNS, 1340–1642

4

SOMERSET TOWNS, 1340–1642

Robert Dunning

It is not easy to define a town as Sir William Savage, writing over forty years ago, discovered. Such a definition, he felt, was not a precisely achievable object, and in cases of doubt there are sometimes sharply differing opinions. Writing about Dulverton in 1901 F.J. Snell remarked that the place was 'only by courtesy a town'. Let courtesy, then, be our defining principle.

In the minds of local tax collectors in 1340 there were, apparently, no doubts. Sixteen places in the county were regarded as either city (*civitas*) or borough (*burgus*). Bath, the only city, came third after Wells and Taunton in terms of the value of the moveable goods of its inhabitants. At the other end of the scale came, in descending order of size, Chard, Weare, Nether Stowey and Watchet. Already since 1327 Somerton had been demoted from the ranks of boroughs. In terms of size, there were 106 taxpayers in Bath in 1340, but no other contempo-

John Speed's map of Bath, 1610, published as an inset of his map of Somerset.

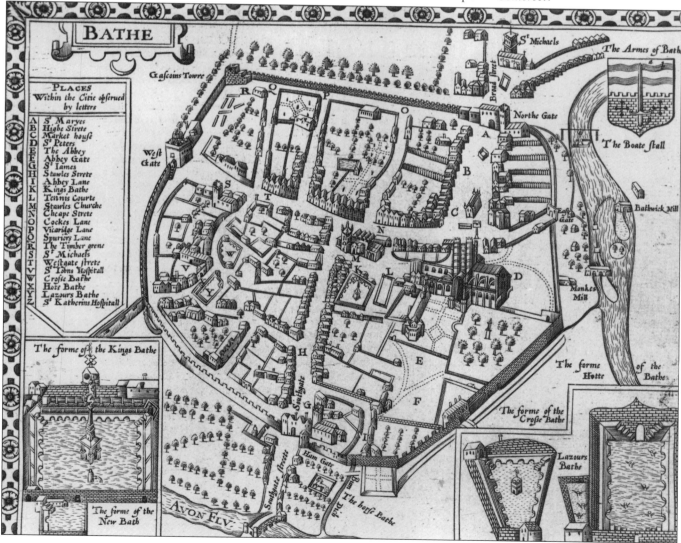

rary lists have survived for the county. For the poll tax of 1377 Bath was still third in size with 570 payers. Bridgwater had moved to second place with 858, Wells was still in the lead with 901 while Taunton had fallen to fourth place with 539. Langport was then half the size of Taunton; Dunster, Stogursey and Ilchester a quarter. Montacute, with 87 tax payers, Stowey and Watchet were all smaller still.

Over a period of 300 years change in relative size is to be expected. When a different generation of tax collectors was charged in 1641 with the difficult task of producing money for another hard-pressed king, Charles I, the record also produces serious difficulties. Minehead followed by Williton appear to be the largest settlements in the county; Taunton borough is closely followed by Wellington; North Curry and Brompton Regis both appear to be larger than Bath. Dulverton's 98 tax payers compare with Bridgwater borough's 84, but hardly with Yeovil's 18 and Langport's 8. To be described as a borough or to have a significant number of tax-paying inhabitants are defining factors, but by no means the only ones. Historical status is another.

Thirteenth-century brass head of the bailiff's staff of the town of Ilchester. It is the oldest surviving staff of office in England and is now preserved in the County Museum.

Somerset's county town, Ilchester, was placed around the middle in the four-teenth-century lists and boasted 14 payers in 1641. About 1370 the gaol at Ilchester became again the county gaol, replacing that at Somerton, and the town was looking forward to potential money-making opportunities from the royal circuit courts and the county sessions which Somerton had enjoyed during the previous century. This potential was largely unachieved: the county gaol remained in the town until 1843 but the gaol sessions were rarely held there and the magistrates only came for Spring sessions from the early seventeenth century. County elections were held there but without enthusiasm: Taunton and Wells were suggested in the early eighteenth century as much more suitable since Ilchester was 'such an odious place that there is neither meat, drink, nor lodging to be had'. The town's own right to send two members to Parliament was suspended between 1361 and 1621.

Wells would have been eminently suitable as a county town on many counts: the seat of the bishop, Somerset's largest town, its central position. Probably one reason against was that it was exclusively ecclesiastical: the bishop, not the king, was lord. Royal charters from John and Edward I confirmed the limited trading privileges given by a succession of bishops from the later twelfth century but apparent alarm at the raising of the walls around the bishop's palace coincided with the appearance of a royal charter in 1341 virtually excluding the bishop from the town, and this did nothing to improve the situation. After protracted litigation the bishop triumphed. The glimmerings of corporate action began to appear in the fourteenth century with the naming first of a steward of the guild and later a 'master of the commonalty' (later mayor) of the borough. The burgesses finally achieved success when the bishop's power was in decline. Letters patent of 1589 incorporated the mayor, masters and burgesses of the city or borough with a council and a court of record. Henceforth they were masters in their own house.

The struggle for independence at Wells lasted for nearly three centuries and illustrates well the power of ecclesiastical lords. Taunton, under the bishops of Winchester, and Bath, under the control of the prior of Bath, were similarly able to secure corporate self-government only with difficulty. Glastonbury and Bruton fared even worse if legal status and administrative power are the only criteria. But economic size and prosperity are surely others. The high quality buildings of the mid-fifteenth century which have recently come to light in Bruton's High Street combined with contemporary references to local men, mostly in the cloth trade, doing business with merchants in London, Hampshire, Berkshire and Dorset, indicate that the people of Bruton had better things to do than to worry about self-government. The portreeve in office in 1385 and the town bailiff named in 1484 may well have been creatures of the prior across the Brue, but his hand was light. Indeed, the last head of the house, John Ely, went

View of Wells from the south-west, after a drawing by W.W. Wheatley, c 1840. St Cuthbert's Church and Wells Cathedral dominate the scene.

View of Bruton, by J. Buckler, 1845.

to the no doubt considerable expense of building a fine market cross in the centre of the town and of acquiring royal licence for two new fairs! As landlord he would undoubtedly have benefited from increased tolls and the place which in 1540 was 'much occupied' with cloth-making was at the time importing through Bristol woad from the Azores for two fullers, wine for a vintner and iron and oil for four smiths.

Glastonbury's history as a town over the same period is more curious. The dominance of the abbey might reasonably be assumed, while the six men who

The junction of High Street and Magdalene Street, Glastonbury. Unsigned watercolour, c 1800.

described themselves in 1319 as burgesses, when declaring to the bailiff of Bridport that Richard le Sleghe was honest, may simply have been giving themselves a status they did not dare to use at home. In that same year a writ addressed by the Crown to the bailiff of the abbot's liberty to send two representatives to a parliament was neither returned nor repeated. Yet, perhaps following the lead of the churchwardens of St John's parish who, from the late thirteenth century, had corporate property and, from 1334 or earlier, a common seal, the community of the town were, by 1349, using a common seal of their own while in 1448 they accepted from the abbot and convent a grant of land to be converted to an archery practice ground. The distinction may have been more cosmetic and political than real. The rent for the land was to be paid by the churchwardens. The failure of Sir John Sydenham's proposal to the House of Commons in 1554 that Glastonbury become Somerset's county town ensured that the real rulers of Glastonbury, in spite of the creation of a corporation in 1705, were, until 1835, successive churchwardens. Yet during this same period the town was prosperous enough, producing from the later sixteenth century a variety of woollens, worsteds and serges and, from the 1620s, stockings.

By that time Bridgwater was in relative decline, the consequence of a changed and changing pattern of national and international trade. The town could reasonably date its emergence as a self-governing community to the charter granted by King John to William Brewer in 1200. Independence as created by incorporation was, curiously, achieved by a charter granted in 1468 ostensibly because of the town's decline. Its economic prosperity, based largely on overseas trade, principally in cloth and wine, seems not to have been affected by the change and to have remained at a high level until the 1540s. By the early seventeenth century, when trade again revived significantly, business was almost entirely coastal, the wine, for instance, coming via Bristol rather than directly from France and Spain. Bridgwater was still the largest port in the county.

Overseas trade and command of the River Parrett clearly gave Bridgwater a position which the county's smaller ports lacked, and of these only Watchet had any claim to urban status between the fourteenth and seventeenth centuries. This was based less on the rather vague use of the words borough and burgage

and more on land held by the community of the borough in the 1360s, the pattern of streets around a market place in the fourteenth century, and busy trade in French wine and Welsh cattle and coal by the beginning of the seventeenth century. Langport's position as an inland port has curious similarities. It sent members to three parliaments compared with Watchet's one; a reeve or portreeve was concerned with commonalty land and the town still reveals a pattern of burgage tenements. Because of the barrier created by Bridgwater bridge, all goods for the upper Parrett (as also for the Tone and Taunton) had to be transhipped and to an extent controlled, but in the mid-fifteenth century Langport had become a considerable importer of woad through Southampton.

Yet it was essentially around markets that towns developed, either naturally in the sense of the topographical advantage of place, or by design. Taunton's natural position in its fertile vale was established well before Domesday, the focus of the vast local estate of the bishops of Winchester. Crewkerne, too, with a pre-Conquest mint and a Domesday market, was already well established by the fourteenth century. Milborne Port similarly had a market at Domesday which by the early thirteenth century was administered by townsmen. Axbridge was also a significant royal borough at Domesday and its men were privileged by King John and its market and fairs were its life-blood.

A covered wagon entering the Vale of Taunton Deane, by Thomas Rowlandson, c 1800.

The medieval market cross and the Church of St John the Baptist, Axbridge, after a painting dated 1756.

The subsequent history of those four places illustrates well the variety of urban experience. The importance of its market kept Taunton one of the leading towns in the county though without many of the characteristics of self-government that local businessmen elsewhere would have considered essential. The townsmen of Crewkerne seem only to have acted collectively from the later sixteenth century and the town's prominence came about in the earlier seventeenth century thanks to the acumen of Thomas Hutchings, the postmaster, the first to make a profit out of his business. Milborne Port's failure to achieve greatness is accounted for by the economic success of its neighbour Sherborne. It seems that it was almost by accident that the Domesday borough was not forgotten. Between 1298 and 1307 the town sent representatives to five parliaments, in the later fourteenth century there was a guild merchant and in the 1430s two borough bailiffs had control of a common seal. The revival of the parliamentary franchise at Milborne Port, as at Ilchester, in the early seventeenth century, while notionally based on precedent, was no reflection of economic importance but simply an opportunity for two local politicians to increase their influence. Axbridge was too near Wells (and subsequently shared a lord) to be a serious rival.

The proximity of competing settlements was clearly a problem. Thomas Gerard was convinced that Yeovil prospered because of the failure of Stoford, itself a speculative venture of the thirteenth century which took advantage of the river crossing into Dorset and probably of the disarray that regularly afflicted Yeovil's corporate affairs. Other new settlements of that kind, where a landlord was attracted by the prospect of cash rents and market tolls from burgage tenants, include the long-term failures of Southwick in Huish Episcopi and Newport in North Curry. Who with any common sense would establish a business on a road going nowhere little more than a river's breadth away from Langport or on a rather wet site so near North Curry?

Nature, or at least the *status quo*, can sometimes be improved upon. The lord of Somerton in the later thirteenth century laid out a market place on the south side of the settlement and successfully diverted the main road from its ancient

The junction of Middle Street and Union Street, Yeovil, c 1910, showing the medieval building (since demolished) known successively as the Higher Three Cups, the White Hart and the Castle Inn.

The town hall and market cross, Somerton, by W.W. Wheatley, 1845.

course to bring in business. Similarly, in the early thirteenth century the lord of Chard manor laid out a borough beside the road that was developing as an important thoroughfare to the north, the same road from which Crewkerne, Yeovil and Sherborne benefited. And, to prove its success, the little borough sent members to several parliaments between 1313 and 1328. But, despite some further progress like the appearances of royal justices, a corporate seal bearing the date 1570 and a mayor, that essential thoroughfare had bypassed the town by the later seventeenth century.

Whether by accident or design several charters of the sixteenth or earlier seventeenth century seem to have revived earlier market grants and began a

process of town creation which included an element of public service. Thus the lord of Wincanton manor had received a market grant in 1235 and a borough had been mentioned in 1345 when market and borough could only be defined as a collection of burgages in the centre of the settlement. Yet in 1554 the town (the word used in the grant), acting as a corporate entity, secured a royal charter to hold a market each Wednesday and fairs on the Tuesday after Easter and on 22 July. Thereafter market and fairs were administered by a body of trustees who probably owned and rented out butchers' shambles in the market place and may even have provided market accommodation which later became a market house. Only after the town found itself on the main route between London and

The harbour at Minehead. Unsigned watercolour, c 1800.

Plymouth by the later seventeenth century did the market trustees find water-supply and fire-fighting on their agenda.

Dulverton's lord had a grant of a Thursday market and a three-day fair in 1306. Market and a successor fair had lapsed by the sixteenth century, so in 1555 John Sydenham, the lord of the place, and nine other named inhabitants became charter trustees of a Saturday market and two fairs. Here, public utility was specified: profits were to be used for the benefit of the inhabitants and the trustees were to be a perpetual body. The purpose of the charter was quite evident: the place was in 1555 'very populous and in decay'. In a lawsuit heard in 1594 it was stated that the constables of Dulverton had normally collected the market tolls and rents, that the trustees had accounted annually to the parish, and that the profits had been spent on building shambles, relieving the poor and equipping men for military service. Dissenting voices declared that instead of money and clothing for the poor there were 'apples, pears and whitbread'. The 'industrious poor' were still in receipt of profits in the eighteenth century.

A third case was Langport which in 1563 clinched its urban status. Its portreeve and commonalty obtained a charter acknowledging ancient rights and confirming market and fair tolls for the express purpose of repairing bridges. A second charter, granted in 1616, incorporated the governing body, set up the paraphernalia of urban administration and authorized the collection of tolls. Another, not quite contemporary, recipient of a charter was Castle Cary. Thomas Gerard recorded a Tuesday market held 'anciently' which had long lapsed and was 'lately renewed' by the earl of Hertford, but it was 'none of the greatest, hardly of the middle size'. The date of the charter is unknown but the earl died in 1621 and the market house of 1616, still standing in Collinson's time (1791), suggests that the earl was serious in intent.

Portrait of Elizabeth I at the beginning of Minehead's charter of incorporation, 1559.

Wincanton, Dulverton, Langport and Castle Cary may serve as the latest examples of urban revival in a county already amply endowed with towns. The example of Minehead combines revivalist aspirations with a stronger statement of public responsibility than that accepted by most ancient urban corporations. The charter granted in 1559 was for rebuilding Minehead's silted-up harbour and reviving its business, in decline because of war. The creation of an incorporated free borough with powers stretching from Porlock to Watchet could not by itself cure economic depression and a less than sympathetic lord with the money to build a new harbour on a different site was instrumental in the withdrawal of the charter and the collapse of self-government. But the new harbour and the town prospered.

Formal urban status, as the evidence from Somerset so often suggests, does not necessarily make a town, but formal written records help to establish what topography and economic realities might otherwise make seem improbable. The absence of such records means that, for instance, little or nothing can be said with confidence of Frome, Ilminster or Wellington as likely urban centres in the period under review. It is not a question of discourtesy; the probabilities are in their favour. So many claimants to urban status in a relatively small area, and radical changes in the lines of roads and means of transport, have resulted in an ever-shifting scene over the three centuries surveyed here. The cloth industry and the seaside were to alter the scene even more. Still, at the end of the twentieth century, let tradition and courtesy guide our understanding rather than simple acceptance of the spurious 'boroughs' created by local government reform in 1974.

SOMERSET AND
THE CIVIL WARS

5

SOMERSET AND THE CIVIL WARS

David Underdown

Never in their history have Somerset people been as divided as in the seventeenth century. Disputes about the proper ordering of Church and State exploded in civil war during the 1640s, and were only resolved after the Monmouth Rebellion and the Glorious Revolution. Most people wanted to live in peace with their neighbours, but a few were willing to fight and die for their beliefs. When civil war came, their often reluctant countrymen were engulfed with them in the struggle.

When did it all start? In the reign of Henry VIII, some would say, when the first stage of a reformation of the Church not only led to bitter disputes over religion, but also helped to establish a new governing class of county gentry. Many of the gentry did very well out of the sales of monastic estates and from service to the Crown. Well-educated and self-confident, they expected their monarchs to listen to them, which the Stuart kings, who reigned after 1603, were unwilling to do. In the 1620s the most vocal of the Somerset gentry was Sir Robert Phelips, whose father had built a glorious mansion at Montacute. In the parliaments of that decade Sir Robert repeatedly denounced the corruption and misgovernment of Charles I's unpopular chief minister, the Duke of Buckingham. The king himself was still above criticism. 'We come with loyal hearts,' Phelips declared in 1628; 'his majesty shall find that it is *we* that are his loyal councillors.' 'We':

The Great Chamber, Montacute House, as it may have appeared in the time of Sir Robert Phelips, after a sketch by C.J. Richardson.

the honest, independent country gentry, not the self-interested, immoral courtiers. Measures like the Petition of Right were intended to protect the 'ancient constitution', not to deprive the king of his just prerogatives. And as a Somerset JP, Phelips conscientiously maintained the king's authority – though in the process often striking a shrewd blow at his local rival, Lord Poulett of Hinton St George.

In the contentious 1620s the idea of civil war was inconceivable. And after Charles I began his eleven years of 'personal rule' in 1629, criticism of government inevitably became more muted. We should not mistake silence for support – Phelips, for example, skillfully organised a covert campaign against the king's unpopular exaction, Ship Money, simply on the basis of technicalities such as the size of local assessments. But Somerset, like other counties, was for the first time experiencing a modern centralising government: one that imposed more regular, more efficiently-collected taxes than people had been accustomed to. Inevitably there was resistance. By 1640, when Charles demanded men and money for war against his rebellious Scottish subjects, there was a taxpayers' strike and something close to a breakdown of government.

Somerset folk of every social level were united in opposition to Ship Money. In 1638, the grand jury at Bath Assizes spoke for them by denouncing 'the great and heavy taxations by new invented ways upon the country.' They were soon to divide over the problem of who, King or Parliament, was ultimately sovereign, but until 1641 that was beyond their mental horizons: lawful government, after all, was by both.

An exuberant late-sixteenth century communion table in St Michael's Church, Minehead, by S.G. Tovey, 1844.

On the other great issue of the day they were much less united. During Elizabeth I's reign the great conflict with Catholic Spain had identified the Protestant cause as that of national independence, and the defeat of the Armada confirmed that the kingdom had been divinely favoured for standing firm

against the Pope's 'evil empire'. But even Protestants who believed that the English were God's elect still disagreed over whether the recent reformation was a sufficient one. Some felt that in the rituals of the Church of England there remained too many vestiges of 'popery and superstition', and that both Church and Government were excessively permissive about the moral state of the laity. One major issue was the legitimacy of church ales, those drunken versions of the modern parish fete which helped to pay for the upkeep of local churches. At the 1633 Assizes many of the JPs protested at a Whitehall order to tolerate these ungodly revelries.

People who wanted to suppress church ales and other allegedly licentious holidays – and also to clamp down on drinking, sabbath-breaking and other forms of vice – were known as Puritans. They were a powerful movement within the church, and they believed that they, not the ritualistic followers of Archbishop William Laud, represented the true Anglican orthodoxy. They had strong views about the placing of the communion table. Should it be left in the body of the church, in the familiar Protestant way, or railed off in the chancel like a popish altar? The bishop ordered the Beckington churchwardens to rail it in. They refused and went to prison.

Puritans were strongly entrenched in several Somerset towns, and in the cloth-manufacturing parishes in the north-east of the county. But they made little headway in South Somerset. Around Yeovil, church ales and ungodly spectacles such as bear baiting continued to flourish well into the seventeenth century. The rowdy festive culture also survived in parts of West Somerset: at Langford Budville, church ales were held right down to the Civil War. And the cathedral influence ensured that the Puritans achieved little at Wells. There was a spectacular church ale there in 1607, with an accompanying procession containing ribald lampoons on the local Puritans.

*

When civil war came in 1642 the county divided much as it had over religion and morality. The puritan northern parts supported Parliament, the southern and western parishes the King and the Church which had tolerated their traditional festivals. The precipitating cause of civil war was a constitutional one: who should control the army needed to suppress the recent rebellion in Ireland? By the spring of 1642 many MPs felt that they could no longer trust Charles I with the militia power, and made the unprecedented claim that his authority could be over-ridden by parliamentary action. Anxious country folk, in Somerset as elsewhere, now faced the dilemma of which of the two powers – both legitimate parts of a lawful, governing whole – they should obey.

Most of the county's governing élite, whatever their earlier views on Ship Money and church ales, decided that for the sake of law and order they must support the king. Lord Poulett, Sir Ralph Hopton, Sir John Stawell, and many other former critics of the court all became Royalists; a minority, though an important one because it included such men as Alexander Popham, Sir John Horner, and the wealthy clothier John Ashe, took the side of Parliament. For nearly all of them the choice was heavily influenced by religion, with the

Plaster frieze in the Great Hall of Montacute House depicting a skimmity ride. Drawing by Richard Walter, c 1850. A hen-pecked husband is beaten by his wife, then paraded around the village as an object of derision. The victim is evidently providing his own musical accompaniment.

Sir Ralph Hopton (1598–1652) of Witham Friary.

Royalists wishing to preserve an only minimally-reformed Church of England, and the Parliamentarians more sympathetic to the Puritans. But there were exceptions. Hopton was puritan in religion, yet became a distinguished royalist general. Like most of his friends, he saw the war as primarily a political one between the forces of law (the King) and disorder (the Parliament).

A constitutional dispute could be resolved by compromise. A religious one, in which the adherents of each side were convinced that they were fighting God's cause against Satan's, could not. And that is how the Civil War increasingly appeared. 'Religion', Oliver Cromwell reflected, 'was not the thing at first contested for; but God brought it to that issue at last.' There is a striking contrast between the moderate spirit in which the war was fought at first and the bitterness – and greater religious zeal – of 1644 and 1645. When the Cavaliers (as we can now call them) took prisoners in an early skirmish at Marshall's Elm near Street, Lord Poulett's son urged his men not to 'spill the blood of the poor fellows'. They too were their countrymen. Officers who had fought side by side during the Thirty Years War could never forget the ties that bound them. In the summer of 1643 Hopton and his old friend Sir William Waller found themselves commanding rival armies in Somerset and about to fight a major battle. They exchanged anguished letters, hoping to put an end to what Waller sadly described as 'this war without an enemy'. It was to no avail: a few weeks later their armies met at Lansdown outside Bath in the biggest battle of the war in Somerset.

Religious enthusiasm was never completely absent, even in the early days. After the Roundheads entered Wells in August 1642 they smashed stained glass in the cathedral, looted the Bishop's Palace, and raucously paraded through the streets behind a picture of the Virgin Mary held up on a pike. This fanatical spirit was later more common on both sides. The royalist Sir Francis Dodington was famous for hanging prisoners and other atrocities, and the Roundheads also showed a new vindictiveness. When the defeated Cavaliers broke and fled during the great battle at Langport in July 1645, a roundhead officer, we are told, loudly praised God 'with fluent expressions, as if he had been in a rapture.' Such godly enthusiasm was a long way from the tortured doubts with which men such as Hopton and Waller had gone to war.

*

Space does not permit a detailed account of the fighting, but the major milestones must be mentioned. In August 1642 the Marquis of Hertford rode into Wells to raise Somerset for the king. He received nothing like the welcome he expected, and within a few days was menaced by a great force of countrymen from the puritan north of the county who assembled on the Mendips under the command of Alexander Popham and Sir John Horner. They were poorly armed, yet their numbers were sufficiently intimidating for Hertford to abandon Wells and retreat over the Dorset border to Sherborne. Until the following summer the Roundheads controlled most of Somerset, disturbed by only a few minor outbreaks such as the one near Bruton early in 1643. A royalist scribe there quaintly described the enemy not as Parliamentarians but as 'Batcombites', nearby Batcombe being a notoriously puritan village. Local rivalries – the old suspicion of 'foreigners' in the next parish – were often stronger than ideological divisions.

In the summer of 1643 Parliament's authority was comprehensively destroyed. Hopton marched into the county with an army of sturdy Cornishmen; they were joined by cavalry from Oxford. After Waller had rejected Hopton's peace overtures, their two armies met at Lansdown on 5 July in a bloody, inconclusive battle, famous for the death of the Cornish commander, Sir Bevil Grenville, whose monument still stands on the hilltop. Somerset's northern parishes remained overwhelmingly parliamentarian in sympathy. But a few days after Lansdown, Hopton's army destroyed Waller's at Roundway Down in

Lansdown, near Bath, and the monument to Sir Bevil Grenville, the royalist commander who died in the inconclusive battle fought there.

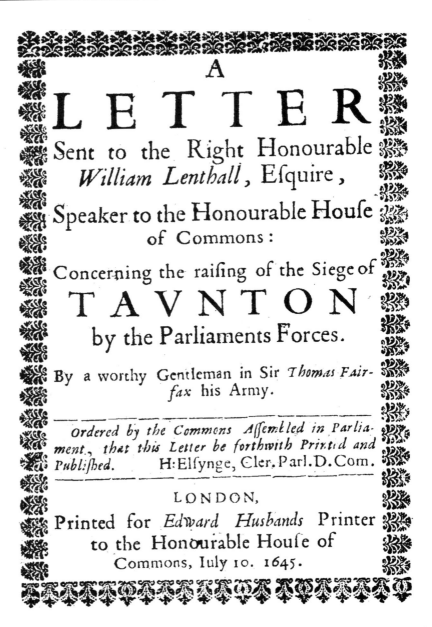

A
LETTER

Sent to the Right Honourable
William Lenthall, Efquire,

Speaker to the Honourable Houfe
of Commons:

Concerning the raifing of the Siege of
TAVNTON
by the Parliaments Forces.

By a worthy Gentleman in Sir *Thomas Fair-*
fax his Army.

Ordered by the Commons Affembled in Parlia-
ment., that this Letter be forthwith Printed and
Publifhed. H:Elfynge, Cler.Parl.D.Com.

LONDON,
Printed for *Edward Husbands* Printer
to the Honourable Houfe of
Commons, Iuly 10. 1645.

Civil War tract describing the raising of the third siege of Taunton, 1645.

Wiltshire in one of the biggest royalist victories of the war. Before the month was out, reinforced by more forces under the king's nephew, Prince Rupert, the Cornishmen stormed Bristol. The Cavaliers had won a complete victory.

For more than a year their control was unchallenged. They tried to govern in the traditional way, but to cope with inevitable wartime demands a new body of commissioners had to be set up. Its members were the traditional rulers of the shire – men like Lord Poulett, Edmund Wyndham, and Sir John Stawell – but with the king breathing down their necks they were less squeamish about taking short cuts to raise the needed money than their JP colleagues were. Early in 1644 they were incorporated in a new 'Western Association' under the command of Rupert's younger and equally ruthless brother, Prince Maurice.

The comparative peace that had prevailed since the summer of 1643 was broken in the following June when the Earl of Essex led a large parliamentarian army into the county. In hot pursuit came the king himself, and both armies made heavy demands – for food, money, and provisions – on the local population. During the next year Somerset endured dreadful suffering, as the rival armies marched and counter-marched, burning and plundering, reducing the inhabitants to ruin and destitution. The worst were the royalist forces commanded by George Goring, himself a stereotypical example of the roistering, irresponsible Cavalier. His men followed his lead, and their 'continual butcheries, rapes and robberies' left deep marks in local memories. Even in the next century, the Bridgwater historian John Oldmixon declared, 'Goring's Crew' were still 'remembered with abhorrence'. The king's young son Charles, the Prince of Wales, was sent to Bristol with a council of respectable advisers to control Goring, but to no avail. The Royalists' chief objective in the spring of 1645 was the capture of Taunton, which had remained in roundhead hands after Essex's march through the county. Stoutly commanded by Robert Blake – later to earn fame as a naval commander – Taunton held out for months against the combined efforts of Goring and other commanders. But a large part of the town

Sir Thomas Fairfax (1612–71), who defeated the royalist army of Lord Goring at the Battle of Langport, July 1645.

The ruins of Bridgwater Castle in the late eighteenth century, after a drawing by John Chubb. The castle was garrisoned by royalist troops under the command of Edmund Wyndham during the siege of July 1645.

was destroyed, and what little remained was in flames when Blake's garrison was relieved on 11 May 1645. The anniversary of the deliverance was long celebrated in Taunton, and the experience cemented the town's self-image as a bastion of godly protestantism.

The military outrages eventually produced a massive protest movement and demands for a negotiated peace. Its supporters, mainly local farmers, were known as 'Clubmen' because they were often armed only with clubs and pitchforks. Clubmen had appeared in Dorset and Wiltshire soon after Goring's arrival in February, 1645, and there was an outbreak in Somerset, in the Brent Knoll area, early in April. It was headed by John Somerset – an appropriate name for the leader of a localist revolt. Both Royalists and Parliamentarians tried to win over the Clubmen. Those from south-east Somerset (always a stronghold of traditional culture) showed more sympathy for the king than for Parliament, but the opposite was true of the Clubmen of the Levels and the adjacent Poldens, who clearly supported Parliament.

On 10 July 1645 Goring was smashed at Langport by Sir Thomas Fairfax's 'New Model' army. Fairfax moved on to besiege Bridgwater, but first he had to negotiate with the Clubmen, who gathered on Sedgemoor and appointed a Woolavington farmer named Humphrey Willis as their spokesman. They offered to support Fairfax if he would restrain his troops from plunder, and after Bridgwater had been stormed they kept their promise. Clubmen assisted Fairfax's army in the campaign leading to the fall of Bristol, gathering on the Mendips in a great assembly very similar to the one that had driven Hertford out of Wells in 1642. Dunster, the last royalist stronghold in the county, surrendered in April 1646: the war was over. Most of the gentry were royalist to the end, but the Clubmen confirm that in central and north Somerset the ordinary folk were generally parliamentarian.

*

The Roundheads quickly forfeited much of their support. Peace provided little relief to a county ravaged by war and its aftermath of plague, economic dislocation and poverty. Somerset people soon groaned under the same burdens that the king had inflicted: high taxes, arbitrary imprisonment, the quartering of soldiers. The chief symbol of this misgovernment was now John Pyne, the puritan squire of Curry Mallet. Pyne dominated the County Committee, the institution through which Parliament governed the localities. The defeated Royalists' estates were sequestered until they paid crippling fines, and they received no sympathy from Pyne. Nor did the clergy who had preached against Parliament or had continued to use the Book of Common Prayer; over a hundred ministers were replaced. But many Parliamentarians also suffered, including the Clubman Humphrey Willis. One famous atrocity was the murder of the former dean of Wells, Walter Ralegh, by the committee's marshal.

There were soon violent explosions against soldiers and the committee's agents. In 1647 the high sheriff, Richard Cole of Nailsea, summoned the inhabitants to meet on Dolebury Warren to resist marauding soldiers. Over much of England in 1648 the dislike of military rule provoked the 'Second Civil War', which merged with an unsuccessful Scots invasion in support of Charles I. Somerset escaped serious disorders, but attitudes were hardening. Pyne's allies were now advocating the overthrow, even the execution, of the king, the 'Man of Blood' responsible, they claimed, for the Second Civil War. Among them were a handful of millenarians who believed that the monarchy would be replaced by a reformed Christian commonwealth, a 'New Jerusalem'. Pyne himself, when named to the court which tried the king, managed to stay away and thus avoided becoming an actual regicide. It saved his neck in 1660.

The Commonwealth which followed the king's execution did nothing to undermine Pyne's control of Somerset, for he swiftly packed the magisterial bench with JPs from his faction. Yet the revolution had surprisingly few effects beyond the change of personnel. JPs continued to maintain law and order, and to supervise the government of the shire, but there were no drastic social or political reforms. The earlier abolition of episcopacy had already undermined eccle-

Charles II, disguised as a servant of Jane Lane, accompanies her on horseback after the Battle of Worcester, 1651. Henry Wilmot follows them. Charles stayed successively at Abbot's Leigh, Castle Cary and Trent before escaping to France.

siastical discipline. Most of the clergy were outwardly Presbyterian (moderate Puritans), but they had to confront a growing number of separatists such as the Baptist Thomas Collier, and a few years later the Quakers. Local people resented intruding outsiders. Cornelius Burges, a well-known Presbyterian, was installed as preacher in Wells Cathedral, but was constantly harassed by the townspeople. And cavalier, Anglican, sympathies always simmered below the surface. In 1651

James Scott, Duke of Monmouth and Buccleuch (1649–85), after a portrait by Sir Peter Lely.

Somerset Royalists played a major part in the escape of King Charles II when, a disguised and hunted fugitive, he passed through the county after his defeat at Worcester. For almost three weeks he was sheltered by Francis Wyndham at Trent, before he eventually reached safety in France.

In April 1653, Cromwell threw out the 'Rump' Parliament which had governed the Commonwealth, and after a brief intermission took over as Lord Protector. The Protectorate was the first stage of a counter-revolution that culminated in the Restoration in 1660. Gradually the old landmarks reappeared – government by a single person, the rule of the traditional governing families in the counties, even a modified House of Lords. It was the end of Pyne's rule, and the county generally welcomed the Protectorate because of its moderation. There was a temporary lurch back into government by the sword after an unsuccessful royalist rebellion in 1655, when Cromwell divided the country into military districts, each ruled by a major-general. Somerset was in the one run by John Disbrowe, a hard-bitten puritan soldier who brooked no opposition or criticism. The experiment was long remembered, strengthening already deep-rooted fears of a 'standing army'. Cromwell abandoned it when its unpopularity became clear; in the 1656 election the slogan 'No Swordsmen!' carried all before it, and in his last years there was at least a pretence of legal government.

*

Oliver's death in 1658 was followed by a period of chaos, but in May 1660 King Charles II returned amid widespread rejoicing. When news arrived that Parliament had voted for restoration, one of the Pouletts counted 142 bonfires within sight of Hinton St George. The Somerset gentry, whatever their previous allegiances, were united in welcoming the Restoration, which for them promised an end to the religious, political, and social upheavals of the previous twenty years. Roundhead Pophams and Horners joined cavalier Pouletts and Wyndhams in sponsoring a 'loyal address' to the restored monarch. But the harmony of 1660 ended when it became clear that both the royalist gentry and their clerical allies wanted revenge, not reconciliation. Just as the

The sweet chestnut, known as the 'Monmouth tree', in Whitelackington Park. During his Western Progress in 1680 Monmouth, attended by an enormous crowd, sat under the tree and touched for the King's Evil. The tree was blown down in 1897.

*The George Inn, Norton St Philip.
Unreliable tradition says that the
Duke of Monmouth stayed at the
George before his skirmish with
royalist forces on 27 June 1685.*

Parliamentarians had expelled royalist incumbents in 1646, so the Cavaliers purged the Puritans in 1662. A series of measures – the so-called 'Clarendon Code' – made life difficult for clerical and lay nonconformists alike.

Yet the puritan legacy, represented by the Presbyterians and Congregationalists, survived in the old roundhead towns and villages. At Taunton, the 11 May thanksgiving was annually observed into the next century. Imprisoned nonconformists still got their message to the faithful. One of them used to preach to his flock through the barred windows of Ilchester gaol. In the 1670s opinion became still further polarised. Many feared that Charles II, for all his cheerful cynicism, was bent on introducing the absolute monarchy on the French model that his father had failed to achieve, and that behind this was a scheme to return the country to Roman Catholicism. Such fears deepened when it became known that James, Duke of York, the king's brother and heir, was himself a Catholic. On the other side, supporters of the crown became more intolerant than ever. In 1683 the 'Tories', as they were now called, attacked and destroyed Taunton's nonconformist meeting-houses, burning their furnishings in the market place.

Protestant hopes were focused on James, Duke of Monmouth, the eldest of Charles II's numerous illegitimate children. He was vain and empty-headed, but he saw that by courting the Protestants and their allies, the new 'Whig' party, he might be able to forestall York's succession, and himself become king. The Whigs claimed that Charles II had been secretly married to Monmouth's mother, and that he, not York, was the lawful heir to the throne. Monmouth did little to dissuade them, and in 1680 undertook a great progress through South Somerset, being entertained by the Whig gentry, and greeted by enthusiastic crowds. In 1684, after the failure of an alleged Whig plot to assassinate both Charles and his brother, Monmouth fled to Holland. But he was still remembered among the West Country Protestants, and there was much subterranean talk about his legitimacy.

In 1685 Charles II died, and at first it appeared that his brother's accession as James II had been a peaceful one. But then on 11 June Monmouth landed at

Lyme Regis with a small force and quickly reignited the Protestant enthusiasm of the peasants and clothworkers; 'the people of God', they liked to call themselves. Armed with scythes and pitchforks, they flocked to the duke's army, whose numbers soon grew to several thousands. They marched to Taunton, with its memories of heroic resistance in 1645, and there Monmouth was proclaimed king. The local militia mustered against him, but their feebleness suggests that many of them sympathised with the rebels. The arrival of a royal army quickly changed the situation. Monmouth's ill-equipped men marched wearily around the county, with no clear strategic aim. They were victorious in a skirmish at Norton St Philip, but the incessant rains of an English July soon washed away what was left of their morale.

Monmouth retraced his steps and by 3 July he was in Bridgwater, following rumours that a huge force of Clubmen from the Levels intended to join him. Less than 200 actually appeared, but the report is significant. This was the region where Humphrey Willis's Clubmen had emerged in 1645, and the term still denoted a force of country people united in their hatred of 'Popery and Arbitrary Government'. The story of how Monmouth led his men out of Bridgwater on that fateful night march has often been told. So has the story of the battle which followed, when the ill-trained and disorganised rebels were mown down by disciplined professionals. Less often noted, however, is the fact that the Battle of Sedgemoor was fought in the very place where the great Club meetings in support of Parliament had taken place forty years before. Sedgemoor thus symbolises a popular cause which had endured throughout the century, and its final defeat.

Most of the gentry wisely stayed out of the rebellion. The subsequent atrocities committed by Kirk's soldiers, and at the order of Judge Jeffreys in the infamous Bloody Assizes, reduced the county to abject submission. But old loyalties never entirely disappeared. In 1686, the year after Sedgemoor, there was a riot at Huntspill fair when Monmouth sympathisers from Burnham assaulted the 'loyal

'From the Field of Sedgemoor', after the painting by Seymour Lucas. A fugitive rebel hides following the battle on 6 July 1685.

party'. Meanwhile the new king was showing that fears of his Catholic intentions were not misplaced. He suspended the laws prohibiting the employment of Catholic officers in the army, governed in alliance with a curious coalition of Catholics and nonconformists united only by their dislike of Anglican privilege, and in other ways further antagonised the previously loyal gentry. In 1688 he was overthrown in the Glorious Revolution, and his replacement by William and Mary confirmed the victory of the cause of limited monarchy, of Protestantism and 'Liberty and Property', for which so many people had struggled and died. But in Somerset as elsewhere it was the gentry's version of that cause, not the common people's, which triumphed.

THE AGE OF ELEGANCE

6

THE AGE OF ELEGANCE

Robin Bush

The years between the ravages of civil war and rebellion in the seventeenth century and the reforms of Church and State that characterized the nineteenth century were a period in which the gentry of Somerset increasingly dominated the countryside and, to a lesser extent, the towns. They served as magistrates both locally and at Quarter Sessions; they took their turns as high sheriff; and many represented the county and its ancient boroughs at Westminster as MPs. Above all the gentry wholly dominated the particular areas in which they lived. Secure in the possession of often extensive estates, they continued to hold their manor and sometimes their hundred courts and to control most aspects of the lives led by the farmers and cottagers who were their tenants. In many cases they appointed the clergy who ministered in the parish churches: churches that were often full of memorials to their gentry ancestors and where every Sunday the lord of the manor and members of his family, deliberately segregated from their tenants, occupied the most prominent pew. Indeed the few churches that were rebuilt during these years were financed by landowners largely for their own convenience: Babington for the Longs (1730), Redlynch for the Earl of Ilchester (1730), Berkley probably for Thomas Prowse (1751) and Marston Bigot for the Earl of Cork and Orrery (1789). In short, the whole structure of local society reflected the superiority of the family that lived in the big house.

In the west of the county there was a small crop of local families who had lived on their properties for centuries. The Luttrells of Dunster had held East Quantoxhead manor by descent from an ancestor who had received it from William the Conqueror. They had held Dunster Castle since buying it from the Mohuns in 1375 – although they did not move in until the death of Lady Joan Mohun in 1404 – ruling a substantial estate lying mainly in the lee of Exmoor and the Brendons, and including the parliamentary borough of Minehead. At Nettlecombe, not far away, the Trevelyans had been established since 1481. They were descended in the female line from the Raleghs, lords of the manor since about 1160, and had secured a baronetcy for their support of the royalist cause during the Civil War. At Fairfield in Stogursey the Aclands (later Acland Hoods) held their estates by direct descent from the twelfth-century Goslan. Though the Wyndhams had been settled at Orchard Wyndham near Williton only from the early sixteenth century, they enjoyed their property by virtue of their descent from Thomas Orchard in 1287. Sir William Wyndham (d. 1740) held a succession of major posts under Queen Anne, including those of Chancellor of the Exchequer in 1713 and Chief Treasury Commissioner a year later. Four of his successors were earls of Egremont, a title preserved in the name of a well-known hotel at Williton.

The Carews of Crowcombe were another family with deep roots in West Somerset, and like so many gentry families in the eighteenth century they were also passionate builders. They descended in the female line from Wimond de Crowcombe, lord in the early twelfth century, and had lived below the western slopes of the Quantocks since about 1570. Between 1724 and 1739, Thomas Carew, MP for Bridgwater, demolished the family's old Tudor house beside the parish church and replaced it with a substantial brick mansion, Crowcombe Court, at the end of a long straight drive. He engaged as architect a Devon joiner

The hall, Nettlecombe Court, by S.G. Tovey, 1845.

Fairfield, Stogursey, by J. Buckler, 1836.

called Thomas Parker, who proved an unfortunate choice. Despite considerable expenditure and the felling of six woods on Thomas Carew's other manors, the house remained unfinished. Parker was eventually discharged and Nathaniel Ireson, a Wincanton architect, was brought in to complete the work. Only later was it discovered that Parker had stolen several bags of coin concealed behind panelling in the old house, probably hidden at the time of the Monmouth Rebellion. Parker's accomplice, the plumber, revealed the theft when he imagined himself to be dying, and the money was recovered following a treasure trove inquest held in Carew's own manor court. Even then, the enormous size of the new building afflicted Carew with bouts of what he called 'melancholy' during which he would decamp to one of his smaller properties and try to write either the history of Parliament or the history of Somerset, both of them projects which he never finished. More successfully, he planted out the Quantock hillside above his small deer park, and he and his descendants created a picturesque landscape in the valley behind the house, complete with ponds, cascades, a ruined chapel, a flint bridge (dated 1776) and walks with occasional seats decorated with fossil ammonites.

Some eighteenth-century Somerset families had purchased their estates following the dissolution of the monasteries by Henry VIII. The Horners had established themselves at Mells, near Frome, by 1442 and bought that manor and others formerly owned by Glastonbury Abbey. There is no truth, however, in the story which identifies the original purchaser with the nursery rhyme character, Little Jack Horner. Kelston, near Bath, formerly a possession of Shaftesbury Abbey in Dorset, was settled on a natural daughter of Henry VIII when she married John Harington of London. There the family lived until Henry Harington sold up in 1759 to Sir Caesar Hawkins. Hawkins demolished the Elizabethan mansion of the Haringtons and commissioned John Wood the younger to build the present Kelston Park high above the River Avon. One surviving branch of the Haringtons moved first to Chew Magna and then to Corston, later producing John Harington, a member of the Supreme Council of Bengal. John was, however, chiefly remembered for siring six legitimate children and a further nine illegitimate offspring.

South front of Crowcombe Court viewed from across the park, c 1885.

The stable court, Crowcombe Court, c 1885.

Other landowners were more recent additions to the Somerset scene. The lawyer James Medlycott came from Berkshire to Milborne Port where he succeeded his brother as MP in 1710. To the east of the small town from 1696 he built Ven House, a superb Georgian mansion and the earliest major brick building in the county. The family's political life in the small borough was not always straightforward. The Medlycott efforts to ensure the election of their candidates

Aerial view of Ven, Milborne Port, seat of the Medlycott family.

at the polls included breaking into the Town Hall in 1774 and stealing the borough seal to validate their return. Marriage into the ancient family of Speke was responsible for the arrival at Dillington House, near Ilminster, of Lord North (d. 1792), later Prime Minister and Earl of Guilford. It was marriage, as well, which brought the Jolliffes from Hampshire to Kilmersdon in 1778 where, between 1789 and 1791, James Wyatt created Ammerdown House for Thomas Samuel Jolliffe. At Newton St Loe near Bath in 1666 Joseph Langton, merchant and Mayor of Bristol, bought a country estate to reflect his new-found wealth and success. There between 1762 and 1765 his grandson Joseph Langton built Newton Park, probably designed by Stiff Leadbetter, and described by Pevsner as one of the finest of the century's houses in Somerset. Around it 'Capability' Brown created a parkland setting, which included two lakes, as well as giving a crenellated makeover to the medieval keep and gatehouse of the St Loes.

Fortunes made from sugar and slavery brought a further two Bristol families to the county. Caleb Dickinson (d. 1783), a Quaker merchant from Bristol who had made a fortune from West Indian sugar plantations and slave trading, bought Kingweston near Somerton in 1740. His son William, an MP prominent in county affairs, rebuilt Kingweston House in sober Georgian style in the 1780s, diverting roads and virtually sweeping away the village to create his park. The Bristol Pinneys, who had estates on Nevis, also built up a successful trade in sugar and slaves. In 1799 John Pretor Pinney moved out of Bristol to an estate in Somerton, although the family did not rebuild their mansion, Somerton Erleigh, until 1846. A third family, the Tudways of Wells, prospered as a result of their sugar plantations on Antigua. They preferred a town house to a country mansion, Charles Tudway building the Cedars in the Liberty at Wells between 1759 and 1761. Charles represented Wells at Westminster and members of his

JOHN PINNEY ESQ.
B.1740. D.1818.

John Pretor Pinney (1740–1818) of Somerton Erleigh. Pinney made his fortune as owner of the largest sugar plantations in Nevis.

family continued to hold one of the city's two seats well into the nineteenth century.

The most eccentric piece of house building in the county was carried out between 1751 and 1755 at Enmore at the south-eastern end of the Quantocks. There beside the parish church John Perceval, 2nd Earl of Egmont, obsessed with creating a feudal enclave in rural Somerset, constructed the massive Enmore Castle, complete with dry moat and patent mechanical drawbridge. Around his incredible home he laid out a large park with wonderful views across Bridgwater Bay, a project which led to the removal and rebuilding (out of sight) of much of Enmore village. Mounting debts led to the castle's sale in 1834 and the purchaser, Nicholas Broadmead of Milverton, demolished three-quarters of his extraordinary acquisition.

Inevitably there were also dynasties which died out or dropped down the social scale. The last Rodney to own Rodney Stoke on the Mendips, Sir Edward, died in 1657 leaving only daughters to survive him. Their house was eventually demolished and it was sentiment not property that led his brother's descendant, one of England's great naval admirals, to take the title Baron Rodney of Rodney Stoke in 1782.

*

Just as Thomas Carew and his successors devoted as much effort to creating their park as to building and maintaining the troublesome Crowcombe Court, so other long-established families willingly paid enormous sums for remodelling the

gardens and grounds which surrounded their mansions. Formal gardens, such as those illustrated by Kip and Knyff at Brympton D'Evercy and Orchard Portman were to become things of the past as the eighteenth century ran its course. One of the last such developments was carried out in the 1690s. The young Sir John Trevelyan, soon after taking possession of his Nettlecombe estate, set about creating 'a new canall-pond and a new cascade of five falls or breaks about 26 feet perpendicularr falling in the middle of the said canall', as well as 'new making the garden in the front with a bason for water in the middle'. Little of this survives today because garden fashions changed. More enduring were the barns and stables which he added to many of the farms on his extensive properties. From 1734 Ralph Allen of Bath used the wealth he had accumulated from his highly successful postal service to create Prior Park, a substantial Palladian mansion at Combe Down. Around and below the house he laid out an extensive park mixing the naturalistic planting of trees in clumps with the more traditional avenues. Advised by his friend Alexander Pope, the addition of a gothick summerhouse, cottage and grotto was, perhaps, predictable. Between 1738 and 1754 the 5th Earl of Cork and Orrery similarly laid out his park at Marston House near Frome with two temples, two grottoes and various statues.

Even more elaborate structures were set up by Sir Charles Kemeys-Tynte at Halswell House near Goathurst from the 1750s, including a stepped pyramid ('in honour of a pure nymph'), 'Robin Hood's House', a Doric rotunda (above a concealed ice house) and the recently-restored Temple of Harmony. At Hestercombe House, north of Taunton, Coplestone Warre Bampfylde (d. 1791) created a succession of ponds in the little valley behind the house, an impressive cascade and buildings such as a witch's hut, a Doric temple and a mausoleum, all recently restored. Similar work was carried out at Redlynch for the Earl of Ilchester and at Batheaston. Garden follies reached their most eccentric form at Barwick south of Yeovil. There, by about 1770, the Newman family had set up four elaborate structures at the limits of their park, including the Fish Tower and 'Jack the Treacle Eater'. John Hippisley Coxe (d. 1769) extended and remodelled

Enmore Castle, the feudal folly of John Perceval, 2nd Earl of Egmont, 1783.

his Ston Easton house in Palladian style from 1739 but it was his second son Henry, MP for Somerset, who in 1793 commissioned from Humphrey Repton one of his famous 'red book' designs for the surrounding park. The River Norr was given two new bridges, and a grotto, sham castle and rustic walks were laid out. A further feature which became increasingly popular during the century was the walled kitchen garden as an addition to major houses. Villages

swept away in the late eighteenth century by the landscaping of parks included that at Nettlecombe by the Trevelyans and at Cricket St Thomas by Lord Bridport. The balance was partly redressed early in the nineteenth century by the creation of 'new' villages by the Stephensons at Lympsham and the Aclands at Selworthy.

View of Prior Park, near Bath, c 1750.

*

Ralph Allen (1694–1764), the builder of Prior Park, after a portrait by Thomas Hudson.

It was usually the gentry who supported and occasionally organised the social events – chiefly centred on the towns – that were so important in their lives. There was little sport that we would recognise as such today. The exception, of course, was stag hunting, probably popular on Exmoor long before records begin. Packs of hounds were continuously maintained by the rangers of Exmoor from at least 1598, although the modern tradition was established by Sir Thomas Acland, forester from 1767, who kept the pack which was to become the Devon

The 'mausoleum' in the eight-eenth-century gardens at Hestercombe. The gardens were created by Coplestone Warre Bampfylde from the 1750s onward.

and Somerset Staghounds. More pictorial evidence is supplied by hunting scenes on the late sixteenth-century plaster overmantel in the great hall of Nettlecombe Court and the magnificent seventeenth-century carved staircase at Dunster Castle. Cricket was virtually unknown in Somerset until the nineteenth century and, although there is the occasional reference to tennis courts, it was the game of fives that seems to have been most popular. Purpose-built fives walls survive in association with inns, such as those at the Fleur de Lis at Stoke sub Hamdon and the Lethbridge Arms (formerly the Gore Inn) at Bishops Lydeard, and there were probably many others which have since been demolished. Where no such wall was available the game was regularly played against the tower or a blank wall of the local church, despite opposition from the clergy and church-wardens. Bowls also featured. Thus in 1779 Robert Harris restored a large bowling green behind the Three Cups Inn in Taunton, opening it on three days a week to subscribers and announcing that 'for the better accommodation of his customers and other gentlemen the green is opened Tuesdays, Thursdays and Saturdays.' There are occasional mentions of indoor games such as billiards and shuffle-board in certain inns but the most popular activities in the eighteenth century were cudgel-playing and cock-fighting.

Cudgel-playing was a peculiarly brutal sport in which two contestants belaboured each other with ash sticks, often with one hand tied behind their backs, until blood flowed to within an inch of their eyebrows. Variant forms of the sport in Somerset were also known as butts and cudgels, single-stick or sword and dagger (employing a long and a short stick for each combatant).

Wrestling & Cudgel-Playing.

SEVENTEEN GUINEAS
TO BE PLAYED FOR!

AT WIVELISCOMBE,
On WEDNESDAY the 11th JUNE, 1806,
WRESTLING for 5 GUINEAS.

AT WIVELISCOMBE,
On THURSDAY the 12th JUNE,
Cudgel Playing for 5 Guineas.

AT MILVERTON,
On FRIDAY the 13th of JUNE,
Cudgel Playing for 7 Guineas.

The Play to begin at 2 o'Clock each Day.

☞ *Great Encouragement will be given to Gamesters.*

DRAKE, PRINTER, FORE-STREET, TAUNTON.

Poster announcing wrestling and cudgel-playing at Wiveliscombe and Milverton, 1806.

Indeed, Somerset challenged the 'Rest of the World' at sword and dagger in 1783. Like cudgel-playing, cock-fighting was generally staged at inns whose landlords clearly wanted to stimulate custom. Inter-county contests were common and clearly highly-organised but our knowledge of such occasions is largely derived from advance newspaper advertisements inserted by the 'feeders' and we know little of the breeding, training and staging associated with such encounters.

Artistic activity was less common across the county at this time. The small towns of Somerset could only attempt to provide small-scale versions of such entertainments as were available at Bath. Assembly rooms were built to accommodate balls (usually held to coincide with the full moon because of poor street lighting), card-playing and the occasional concert. Thus Dr Musgrove Heighington, a minor eighteenth-century composer, put on occasional concerts and dances at the Grammar School and Castle Hall in Taunton between 1752 and 1756, attracting performers from as far away as Exeter and Salisbury.

Those living in the north of Somerset would travel into Bath and Bristol to the flourishing theatres and other attractions in those cities, although in 1773 Thornton's company was noted as playing at Chew Magna and Keynsham, as well as further south at Glastonbury and Chard. John Hugh Smyth of Ashton Court, Long Ashton, was a prominent subscriber to the building of a new theatre at Bristol in 1766. Expenditure on lute strings and re-tuning his harpsichord at around the same time shows that he was also providing home-grown entertainment. Elsewhere in the county there were insufficient patrons to support a permanent theatre. Groups of strolling players would set up their stages in inns, halls and assembly rooms and perform their repertoires until attendance began to decline, when they would move on to the next town. Such entertainments tended to follow the Assizes and major fairs, particularly the former, when magistrates, witnesses and others would flock in from all parts of the county and

THEATRE, TAUNTON.

FOR THE BENEFIT

OF THE CELEBRATED

Mr. KEAN,

And the LAST NIGHT of his Engagement.

On FRIDAY EVENING, JULY 25th, 1828.

Will be Performed Massinger's much admired Play of

A NEW WAY
To Pay Old Debts,

The Part of Sir Giles Overeach, by Mr. KEAN,

Wellborn, Mr. BEVERLEY,	Marrall, Mr. FRASER,	Justice Greedy, Mr. WOODS,
Lord Lovell, Mr. KENT,	Allworth, Mr. GORDON,	Tapwell, Mr. YOUNG,
Furnace, Mr. J. DARVIS,	Order, Mr. DAVIS,	Amble, Mr. GILLINGS,
Willdo, Mr. YOUNG,	Tailor, Mr. J. DARVIS,	Vintner, Mr. DAVIS.

Lady Allworth, Mrs. WOODS,   Margaret, Miss LEE,   Froth, Mrs. KENT.

END OF THE PLAY,

Song, "Oysters, Sir," by Miss DARKE,

A favorite Song, by Mr. DAVIS.

The whole to conclude with Coleman's much admired laughable Petite Piece, called

Sylvester Daggerwood

Or, THE DUNSTABLE ACTOR,

Sylvester Daggerwood, by Mr. KEAN,

Fustian, Mr. KENT,   John, Mr. DAVIS,   Servant Mr. GILLINGS,

Doors to be opened at Six and begin at Seven o'Clock.—BOXES 4s.—PIT 2s.—GALLERY 1s.

Tickets to be had of Mr. LEE, at Mr. WEDDON's, Tailor, Paul Street, and at Mr. POOLE's, Printing Office, where Places for the Boxes may be taken, and to prevent mistakes, Ladies and Gentlemen are requested to provide themselves with Tickets.

J. POOLE, PRINTER, TAUNTON.

Poster announcing a performance at the Taunton theatre by Edmund Kean (1787–1833) in 1828.

be accommodated at the many inns that filled the major towns. Thus between 1722 and 1726 Claver Morris, the prominent Wells physician, noted four visits to see plays staged by Lewis and Power's companies at the Crown or the George in Wells, including *The Yeomen of Kent*, *Love for Love* and *The Tragedy of Jane Shore*.

Even in a town such as Langport Thomas Beedall recorded that during the course of a month in 1768 his wife Betsy made ten visits to see plays put on at the Town Hall in Bow Street, on one occasion returning home as late as midnight. At Castle Cary in 1770 Parson James Woodforde similarly enjoyed a month of plays

Scene in the Old Pump Room, Bath, after a painting by G.A. Storey.

in the Court House there. One Shepton Mallet performance in a room over the stables at the Bell Inn in 1779 ended disastrously when the floor collapsed and a young woman was crushed to death.

In the last quarter of the eighteenth century theatres were established in the major towns and individual actor-managers set up circuits of these, often extending into adjacent counties. The most successful circuit was operated by James Biggs, who in 1787 built a theatre (most appropriately) behind the Shakespeare Inn at Taunton, but operated similarly at Bridgwater and Wells, as also at Tiverton, Barnstaple, Lyme Regis and Dorchester. James Shatford, mainly based at Salisbury, joined forces with Henry Lee to licence theatres at Frome and Shepton Mallet in 1794, Wells in 1796 and Bridgwater in 1798. As before, companies would play at particular venues for some three or four weeks and then move on to the next, still following the Assizes whenever possible. It became customary for wealthy individuals to sponsor particular performances and to distribute tickets to their friends and supporters. Towards the end of a run benefit nights would be granted to certain actors or actresses who would receive the profits, rather as prominent cricketers are supported even today. Such circuit players continued to entertain in the rural towns until the mid-nineteenth century when the advent of better communications by road and rail meant that national companies came more regularly and throughout the year. The company which played in Somerset under Henry Lee and his successors was finally wound up after a fire destroyed their theatre, sets and costumes at Bridport in 1843.

*

In its contribution to the social life of the county Bath was of course in a class of its own and served as a magnet to attract well-heeled people not only from Somerset but from all over the country. Although by the seventeenth century Bath had long been accepted as the premier watering-place in England, the Somerset Justices in 1683 still reckoned that Wells possessed better 'accommodation for entertainments'. The visits of Queen Anne in 1702 and 1703 and the advent of Richard ('Beau') Nash, a Welsh professional gambler, in 1705 changed all that. Roads leading into the city were improved and a pump room (1706) and assembly room (1708) were built. Dr William Oliver lauded the qualities of the spa water in 1707 and Nash began to organise social and medicinal activities on a grand scale. Improvements in the quality of lodgings and the exploitation by the architects John Wood and son, and by the entrepreneur Ralph Allen, of the local limestone to rebuild the city in magnificent style established Bath as a social centre to rival even the capital. The advent of a theatre (1729), the Mineral Water Hospital (1738) and circulating libraries gave the place a respectability that tended to conceal the realities of gaming houses and licentiousness on which much of the city's economy depended. A partial decline in the later eighteenth century was aggravated by the growth in popularity of alternative West Country attractions such as the Hotwells at Clifton, the spa attractions of Cheltenham and sea-bathing at Weymouth and elsewhere. Bath, however, was to retain its national and local pre-eminence well into the nineteenth century and, indeed, up to the present day.

ASPECTS OF RURAL LIFE, 1700–1870

15. *The market place and Bekynton's Conduit, Wells, by Edward Dayes, c 1795. Watercolour. Dayes was the teacher of Thomas Girtin, and his style had a great influence on both Girtin and Turner.*

16. *Medieval bridge over the River Tone, Taunton, by Harry Frier, c 1890. Watercolour. The bridge was demolished in 1810, and Frier's watercolour is based on an earlier illustration.*

17. *Gateway to the inner bailey of Taunton Castle, by L.C. Hammett, 1921. Watercolour.*

18. *View of Frome, by W.W. Wheatley, c 1840. Watercolour.*

19. *View from West Quantoxhead towards Watchet and Minehead, by W.W. Wheatley, c 1840. Watercolour.*

20. *Entrance into Mells, by W.W. Wheatley, 1843. Watercolour.*

21. *Cheddar Gorge, by Edward Cashin, 1823. Watercolour. Cashin's style was inspired by seventeenth century Dutch painters, especially Jan van der Heyden.*

22. *Entrance to Cheddar, by Samuel Jackson, 1824. Watercolour.*

23. *Farmhouse at Abbots Leigh, by Francis Danby, c 1822. Watercolour and bodycolour. Danby was a leader of the Bristol School of artists, and painted subjects varying from landscapes to visionary and mythical scenes reminiscent of John Martin.*

24. *Goblin Combe, Wrington, by W.W. Wheatley, 1846. Watercolour. This is among the finest of Wheatley's watercolours.*

25. *Interior of Chew Stoke Inn, by W.W. Wheatley, 1843. Watercolour.*

26. *View at Pill, Easton in Gordano, by W.W. Wheatley, 1843. Watercolour.*

7

ASPECTS OF RURAL LIFE, 1700–1870

Hilary Binding

It has often been said that by the seventeenth century Somerset was one of the largest, wealthiest and most populated counties in England. In 1636 it ranked third, along with Devon, in the Ship Money assessment, while records point to a population of more than 200,000 towards the end of the century. It was a county rich in agriculture and trade, but also a county beneath whose prosperous exterior lurked the growing problem of the poor.

Somerset's physical diversity naturally made for diverse patterns of agriculture. In the north, sheep grazed on the Mendips; teasels (for the woollen industry), barley and oats were grown on the Mendip slopes while in the valley of the river Axe large numbers of cattle were kept, providing milk for the nearby cities of Bath and Bristol and for making cheese. The east and south of the county formed a densely-populated region of small dairy farms with a little corn being grown. Yeovil cheese market was one of the largest in the South West while corn grown in the area about Crewkerne supplied the large market at Chard. In 1633 Thomas Gerard described Martock as 'seated in the fattest part of the Countie, especially for errable which makes the inhabitants soe fatt in their purses.' Supplementary occupations, such as gloving, lace-making and stocking knitting as well as the trades associated with the woollen industry, added to the prosperity of the area.

While Taunton and its surrounding villages in the early eighteenth century could reputedly boast some 1100 looms, it was the fertile Vale of Taunton Deane, with its rich meadows, orchards and arable land, which attracted most attention. Here cattle and sheep were fattened, while fields of barley and wheat marched beside orchards, hop vines and market gardens. Out on the moors open drainage ditches had been dug and maintained since medieval times. Most of the land that still flooded dried out in summer and the covering of water-borne silt created fertile meadows and pasture for dairy and beef cattle. Some corn was grown and incomes were supplemented by fishing, fowling, and cutting reeds and withies. On the Quantocks and the Blackdowns as well as on Exmoor's 'filthy barren ground' a reasonable living could be made from grazing sheep and cattle.

Although the greater and lesser gentry controlled much of the countryside, many independently-minded yeoman farmers – 'wealthy and substantial men though none of the best breed' as Gerard described those at Martock – owned their own farms and lived comfortably. In many places, husbandmen, often copy-holders, rented small, but usually viable, holdings while most agricultural labourers owned a small acreage and a few animals. The changes that were to come over the next 150 years were to alter the lives of many in these two lower categories leaving them with no stake in the land and little independence or status.

Until relatively recently it was thought that the changes that occured in agriculture throughout England and Wales during the eighteenth century were swift and dramatic enough to justify the use of the phrase 'agricultural revolution' – a few inventions, ideas and key figures initiating a rapid change in land-holding and agricultural practice. But this was not the case. Change there was but it came slowly and much depended on the interest or desire for profit of the indi-

Barn at Park House Farm, Donyatt, by W.W. Wheatley, 1850. Threshing by hand provided employment in the winter months.

vidual landowner or farmer. The process of enclosure in Somerset took, at a conservative estimate, over five hundred years and there were still farms in the county in the 1860s which had seen little or no change in management for over a century.

Most enclosure of open fields and common land in the county had taken place by 1700 although in a few places a partial open-field system continued until the end of the nineteenth century and some areas of common and waste were not enclosed until the mid-1800s. Attempts in the seventeenth century to enclose two of the last great unenclosed areas, Selwood Forest on the Somerset-Wiltshire border and Neroche in the shadow of the Blackdown Hills, were delayed by resistance from those holding common rights. At Selwood between 1628 and 1631 'divers lewd and desperate persons' expelled surveyors and at Neroche 'the Rable broke up all the Hedges and Fences and layd all in common again.' Throughout the century attempts to enclose and drain the marshes of the central Levels were frustrated by those eager to defend their rights.

Dr Claver Morris of Wells was a prime mover in the enclosures of Baltonsbury [Baltonsborough] North Wood and Glastonbury Common Moor. They were some of the first Parliamentary enclosures in Somerset and Morris details the difficulties associated with early enclosure and the opposition he met at every stage. There were those who opposed enclosure in Parliament and those who opposed it before the commissioners. There was the man who declared he had never heard that an Enclosure Act had been passed, although legal notices were given out in the proper manner at St John's church, Glastonbury; the suspicious man who was sure he had lost out and that his lots were smaller and contained poorer land than those of his neighbours; the dissenter who insisted on a right of way across the curate's land although another route was offered. Even the representatives of the bishop raised difficulties about the allocation of land to the curate.

Dr Morris became the owner of 41 acres at Baltonsbury having spent about £35 on enclosure there which included making hedges and ditches and levelling 9600 anthills. Once the division of common land had finally been carried out, however, he became concerned for the poorer commoners wondering whether they had been adequately compensated for their lost rights of grazing: before enclosure each commoner could keep a cow or pig and some poultry on the common and the compensation – £5 or £10 – did not go far. Morris set aside £20 which, on 22 December 1722, he distributed at the Rose and Crown to those whom he thought had been unfairly treated.

Objections continued. At Stoke sub Hamdon where there was shared common arable, meadow and pasture, attempts to enclose in 1798 were met by tenants 'so extremely ill-natured that sooner than others should reap any advantage they would forego their own.'

While many poorer people did lose out following enclosure there were others who lost both status and land because of the amalgamation of farm holdings by progressive landowners in attempts to reap economies of scale. John Billingsley writing in 1796 was sure that the consolidation of small farms was essential if agricultural practice and produce were to be improved not only because the larger farmer had more capital to invest but also because 'the ideas of large farmers are more expanded than those of small.' It is interesting to note that some fifty years later small farms were still hindering progress according to Sir Thomas Dyke Acland.

In the 1780s at Norton Fitzwarren, Isaac Welman and William Hawker, lords of the manor, created larger farms by refusing to renew long leases on small and inefficient farms. In Carhampton a similar process was begun by Henry Fownes Luttrell of Dunster Castle in the 1760s and completed by his successor, John, at the end of the century. A process of withholding leases and taking land in hand

A labourer trudges through the churchyard at Carhampton, by W.W. Wheatley, 1845. The shutters may have protected the windows during the playing of fives.

allowed the creation of a new deer park, the enclosure of the old, and the eventual reorganisation of the Carhampton estate. In 1750 there had been thirty-eight small copyholders most with a five-bedroomed house, woodland, arable, pasture and rights in the water meadows and on the seashore and a certain status and independence. By 1795 these holdings had largely been replaced by three large farms; the copyholders became labourers or moved away and the houses were divided into two- or three-bedroomed cottages.

There were farmers eager to put new ideas into practice. In 1765 Burton Pynsent near Curry Rivel was left to William Pitt in gratitude for his action in opposing the Cider Tax. The following year a Mr Speke, perhaps the owner of a neighbouring farm, drew up a plan of action for the farms. He proposed that 300 Dorsetshire sheep should be bought to replace those currently stocked, for 'they will produce more wool and sell better in the Country' while 'mares of the Northamptonshire breed would serve for both coach and plow.' Moortown was to be turned into a dairy farm and Speke suggests that a neighbouring farm be bought to improve the economy of the estate. Thirty years later William Marshall, author of *The Rural Economy of the West of England*, travelling between Taunton and Somerton, was struck by Burton Pynsent which he described as a neat farmery, and large farm, with clean fallows and good clover and farm hedges kept down to fence height. He observed four heavy horses ploughing broken ground as well as six oxen using long, heavy swing ploughs and a full hedgerow of apple trees, all in contrast to the open fields near Langport and Somerton where there was 'foul husbandry', couch grass and thistles.

John Billingsley considered that short leases hindered the progress of farming where they simply laid down the length of the term, the rent to be paid and the course of cropping, and stipulated nothing about the introduction of modern farming methods. Many landowners retained such leases well into the nineteenth century.

When John Knight, an iron master from Wolverley in Worcestershire, bought and enclosed Exmoor Forest in 1818 he determined to reclaim and run the estate himself. However it became clear to his son, Frederic, that the expense of the undertaking was so great that if the whole estate were to be brought under cultivation it needed to be divided into separate farms and let to tenants. Frederic's agent, Robert Smith, offered twenty-year leases with a rising scale of rents and a schedule of allowances for works of improvement attached to each lease. Such improving leases implied a real working relationship between landlord and tenant and were a definite encouragement to investment of capital and better farming.

*

By the 1790s many farm labourers in Somerset were living at or near starvation levels. The problem lay in low wages and the high cost of bread, the underlying cause being the huge rise in population during the eighteenth century; for with so many mouths to feed there was not enough food to go round while pressures of supply and demand forced up prices. A series of bad harvests together with the disastrous economic consequences of war with France led to an unprecedented rise in the price of bread and conditions became so bad that some decided to take matters into their own hands as at Stogursey and Nether Stowey in 1801.

In 1795 in Stogursey families with up to five children were attempting to live on just over eight shillings a week and poor people like Matthew Grose of

The old market house at Nether Stowey, by W.W. Wheatley, 1845. Demonstrators protesting about the high price of provisions met here in 1801.

Dodington died of hunger and were buried 'on the parish'. In a petition prepared by West Somerset demonstrators it was stated that in 1801 a man's average wage was 1s 2d a day while the price of a quartern loaf (which could easily be eaten by one man in a day) was 1s 1d. With wages so low the labourer and his family had to turn to the parish for support and overseers' accounts for many Somerset parishes show huge increases in payments to the poor resulting in corresponding increases in the poor rate. By 1800 some overseers were buying in food and selling it to the poor at less than cost while others supplemented the men's wages and so took away any incentive for the farmer to raise wages himself. Sometimes there was no money to help.

William Wordsworth, living at Alfoxden on the Quantocks in 1797, describes the situation in *The Last of the Flock*, a poem probably based on a reminescence of the Nether Stowey tanner, Tom Poole.

'Six children, Sir, I had to feed;
Hard labour in a time of need!
My pride was tamed, and in our grief
I of the parish asked relief.'

Refused help, the poor smallholder gradually sold off his sheep to buy food.

'As fine a flock as ever grazed!
Upon the Quantock hills they fed.'

There were those who blamed the farmer. William Jenkin, the Duke of Buckingham's agent at Dodington copper mines near Nether Stowey, placed responsibility for the 'enormous advanced price of the necessaries of life' largely at the door of 'the unfeeling, Inhuman and Rapacious dispositions of your over-grown farmers, whose hearts I have often thought are too callous to admit of the least sense of feeling for the suffering of the starving poor around them.' The Rev. William Holland of Over Stowey wished he could 'prevail on the farmers to sell their wheat to the parish at the rate of ten shillings a bushell' – prices were rising to twenty shillings and more at Taunton market – 'and then keep the poor to their usual standard of allowance.' But he has criticism for the poor as well: 'They expect to be kept in idleness or to be supported in extravagance and drunkenness. They do not trust to their own industry for support. They grow insolent. Subordination is lost and [they] make their demands on other people's purses as if they were their own.'

The poor box at Whitchurch, by W.W. Wheatley, 1843

An added pressure during these years was the shortage of labour while men were away fighting in the Napoleonic Wars. While parishes struggled to keep the families the soldiers left behind, some farmers turned to machinery to solve their problems. At North Brewham near Milborne Port a sale brochure dated 1813 noted that in a barn in one of the fields there was a threshing machine that belonged to the tenant, Giles Cox. In that same year a threshing machine was installed for Mr P. Dore at Bridge Farm, Williton, the Earl of Egremont supplying the timber for the water-wheel, shaft and 'feeders and planch' as well as paying masons and carpenters for building the wheel. The total cost of the work was £79 13s which included sawing, hauling wood and 'sinking the river'.

As men returned from the wars looking for work, threshing machines took the brunt of the anger of agricultural labourers who had relied in the past on thresh-ing as a source of employment at the hardest time of year. Whether the condi-tions in Somerset were as bad as in other parts of southern England is not clear but certainly the rioting in 1830–1 attributed to 'Captain Swing' occured only minimally in the county although special constables were sworn in, at Cossington for example, to deal with potential trouble. On 26 November threats were made to destroy a threshing machine at South Brewham – was this the one installed by Giles Cox? – and inflammatory handbills were distributed in Taunton the next day. At Banwell on 30 November there was a riot by paupers in the poorhouse followed by an attack on the lockup and the release of prisoners. Farmers took action to stave off rioters and at Frome, on the same day, a farmer set fire to his own threshing machine while on 1 December Lord Egremont's steward wrote from Ilton that 'for miles around, the farmers and owners have all taken down & destroyed all [threshing machines] that are in the neighbourhood.' Later that day two machines were broken up by labourers at nearby Yenston and Henstridge. There was little more than unrest in the years that followed although in 1834 a paper signed simply 'North Curry' and 'Stoke St Gregory' was circulated in that area offering to burn the ricks of local 'jentelmen' and farmers. By this time agricultural labourers were not looking back to a time when they managed their own plots of land but wanted simply to receive an adequate wage, regular employment and, in some cases, a greater recognition of their worth.

The crux of the problem was over-population: too many labourers looking for too few jobs. The Poor Law Amendment Act of 1834, which established unions of parishes, each with its own workhouse, cracked down on those in need of poor relief, insisting that they should only be supported in the workhouse. A movement to assist the poor devised by Bishop Law encouraged the setting up of allotments and by 1851 these could be found in most parishes. During the eighteenth century friendly societies were established in many parishes to provide mutual help in times of sickness and death but societies often failed because of poor management, lack of funds and, in many cases, because of their close links with the local public house where money could be spent all too easily. In the 1820s and '30s several new friendly societies were set up in Somerset by 'the benevolence of the Superior Orders, co-operating with the provident frugality of the Working Classes.' The North Somerset Friendly Society established in 1827 boasted patron, president, trustees and a general committee consisting of all the resident clergy of the eighteen parishes involved. The Rev. J.J. Toogood, Vicar of North Petherton from 1836 to 1850, founded a new club 'not in opposition to

The blacksmith's shop at Monkton Combe, by W.W. Wheatley, 1850. The font, seen on the left, was moved from the parish church about twenty years earlier.

the old but from a conviction that the present club cannot afford to pay its members at an age and at a period when help is more likely than ever to be needed.'

Hannah More and her sister, Martha, had more ambitious ideas. They had settled near Cheddar in 1789 and begun a programme of Christian education for both children and adults in an area notorious for its violence, depravity and poverty. Three years later Hannah wrote to her friend, William Wilberforce, 'Finding the wants and distresses of these poor people uncommonly great ... it occurred to me that I could make what I had go much further, by instituting clubs or societies for the women, as is done for the men in other places.'

Some people, often the most able with a little capital and who could see a brighter future elsewhere, decided to emigrate encouraged by the government, emigration societies and local parish officials. Agents advertised free passages to Australia for married agricultural labourers, mechanics and single women while James Wilcocks of Plymouth who had agents in Bridgwater, Taunton, Chard and Crewkerne offered cheap passages to New York and Quebec. Some years earlier, in April 1837, 33 people had left Banwell for Quebec with the help of funds from the Exchequer Loan Office in London. In some cases support was provided for emigrants from the parish rate. James England of Chard, his wife Harriet, and their four children were given five pounds to help them on their way to Adelaide in 1854. George Hall Peppin of Dulverton, who is remembered for the merino sheep that bear his name, left for Australia in 1850 after financial responsibilities and a drop in income led to ever-increasing debts.

Church and cottages at Banwell, c 1840.

By 1851 the number of landed proprietors in Somerset was 1873 while there were 8438 farmers. There were 8500 farm servants living in, and 37,000 agricultural labourers earning a weekly wage of between eight and ten shillings augmented by a cider allowance and occasionally a 'bonus' at hay making and harvest. The independent husbandmen of the 1700s had been absorbed into the

*Cider in store at Barrington
Court, 1922*

lowest class; that of the poorly-waged labourer. With wages so low it was necessary for the whole family to turn to. Boys, and girls, sometimes as young as five
or six, spent lonely days scaring birds from the crops; women worked not only
at the busy times of haymaking and the grain harvest but doing back-breaking
tasks such as weeding, picking potatoes and trimming turnips.

In his study of the agriculture of the county published in 1851 Thomas Dyke
Acland presented a varied picture of progress. In general, standards were not
high 'nor the produce of the soil ... all it might be', but throughout the county
individuals were singled out for their good practice and innovative ideas. Mr
Blake at Venne House on Brendon Hill had made great improvements to his
pasture by draining, liming and sowing selected grasses; Francis Quartly of
Molland on the Somerset border had bred such excellent Devon cattle that in
1831 his nephews were able to scoop all eleven prizes at the Exeter show. Mr
Salter, a tenant of Lord Poulett near Crewkerne, was remarkable for the excel-
lence of his implements. 'He has water power, with which, in addition to the
ordinary farm operations, he crushes bones; a drying kiln for corn; a well
selected set of field implements including Chandler's liquid-manure drill, with
one of Hornsby's drills, and the best scarifiers, pressers, ploughs and harrows.'
The Rev. Mr Plucknet farming his glebe at Horton on 'bad land at a great eleva-
tion' had experimented successfully with growing wheat alternately with
vetches and mangold wurzels, had introduced implements suited to the wants of
the small farmer and induced his neighbours to use bones as fertiliser for their
turnips.

Acland's essay was written for the journal of the Bath and West Society which
had been established in 1777 and had played a significant part in the encourage-

WELLINGTON, WIVELISCOMBE, AND MILVERTON
ASSOCIATION.

THE
PLOUGHING MATCH
FOR 1848,

WILL TAKE PLACE IN TWO PIECES OF LEY NEAR THE

WEST TURNPIKE GATE, WIVELISCOMBE,

On FRIDAY, the 13th. day of OCTOBER next, at Nine o'Clock in the Forenoon,

WHEN THE FOLLOWING

PRIZES WILL BE AWARDED:

CLASS 1.
PLOUGHMEN AND BOYS.

To the Labourer or Servant of a Subscriber, who shall Plough with any number of *Horses*, Half an Acre of Land within 3½ hours, with the greatest skill, ...£3 0 0

To the second best, ... 2 0 0
To the third best, ... 1 10 0
To the fourth best, ... 1 0 0
To the fifth best, ... 0 10 0

To the Boys, under 16 years of age who shall drive for the respective Persons who shall obtain the above Prizes :—

To the first, ...5s.
To the other four, ...2s. 6d. each.

CLASS 2.
PLOUGHMEN AND BOYS.

To the Labourer or Servant of a Subscriber, under 20 years of age, who shall plough with any number of *Horses*, Half an Acre of Land, within 3½ hours, with the greatest skill, £1 10 0

To the second best, ...£1 0 0
To the third best, ... 0 10 0

To the Boys under 16 years of age, who shall drive for the respective Persons who shall obtain the last mentioned Prizes :—

To the first, ... 5s.
To the other two, ...2s. 6d. each.

CLASS 3.
PLOUGHMEN AND BOYS.

To the Labourer or Servant of a Subscriber, who shall Plough with any number of *Oxen*, Half an Acre of Land, within 4 hours, with the greatest skill, ...£2 10 0

Second best, ... 1 10 0
Third best, ... 0 15 0

To the Boys under 16 years of age, who shall drive for the respective Persons who shall obtain the last mentioned Prizes :—

First, ...5s.
Second, ...2s. 6d.
Third, ...2s. 6d.

SUBJECT TO THE FOLLOWING CONDITIONS ;—

Each Ploughman is to fit his own Coulter after he is in the Field ; and to plough the Land by gathering one third, and throwing abroad two thirds of the Half-acre.

The Plough, Horses, or Cattle, to be the Property of the Master of the Competitor ; and each Ploughman to have been in his Master's employ at least six months next preceding the day of competition.

No Strings or other unusual means to be used as a Guide for the Work.

ment of good agricultural practice until the 1840s and was undergoing a revival. Meanwhile local agricultural societies and shows such as that at Ilminster were being set up 'for the rewarding of skill and the encouragement of industry and good behaviour amongst agricultural labourers and domestic servants.' Prizes were offered for the best potatoes, onions, parsnips and carrots grown in gardens or allotments; for the best fat pig, for long service, for the largest families brought up without recourse to parochial relief and for abstinence from alcohol. At Chard the Cottagers' Horticultural Society held an annual show, while the first ploughing match took place at Combe St Nicholas in 1854. Soon sheep shearing, turnip hoeing, mow making and thatching of corn joined the list of competitions. When Dunster Show, established in 1835, celebrated its silver jubilee the Show schedule listed 22 classes; 16 for oxen and cattle, three for sheep and rams, two for pigs, four for horses and three for roots.

How much depended on the individual landowner and farmer is made clear in the 1867 Report into the Conditions of Women and Children in Agriculture. Butcombe was described as 'out of the way and neglected' with many non-resident owners and still let in very small holdings. There was an atmosphere of apathy, hopelessness and superstition and a belief in witchcraft, while the lack of education was rife. The cottages were, in general, in a very bad condition and there was no water supply, drainage or ventilation. Few cottages in the village had more than one sleeping-room for father, mother, children of both sexes and sometimes a lodger as well. There were few gardens and no allotments. The vicar, the Rev. W.H. Cartwright, had begun a programme of improvements, pulling down the worst cottages and building new ones, putting up a school and provision for a schoolmistress and founding a clothing club to help the poorest families. His next project was to restore the church.

Old cottages did not necessarily mean bad cottages. One at Staple Fitzpaine, built of cob and thatch was neat and warm. It was once half of an old farmhouse,

Interior of a cottage at Oare, by W.W. Wheatley, 1849. The artist, in the background, noted that 'the old Woman, after frying some Bacon & Eggs, placed a wooden trencher on the table upon which she placed the hot Frying pan & its contents and from which the Driver & Guide helped themselves.'

Design No. 1.

Ground Plan

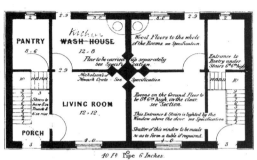

Chamber Plan.

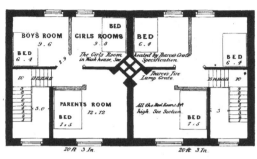

Scale ⅛th of an Inch to a Foot.

The arrangement of Rooms in this Plan offers (among others) the following advantages.

1st The Porch or Entrance prevents the cold draughts which are the certain consequence of the door of the Living Room opening at once into the Air

2nd The Economy of Heat resulting from the arrangement of the Flues

3rd The separation of the Pantry from the rest of the House so as to afford a repository for Meat &c free from the Steam of the Washhouse or the fumes of the Living Rooms.

4th An Easy, light and wide Staircase.

Some of the advantages of this arrangement, are,

1st The division of the Sexes so essential to decency & morality.

2nd Each of the smaller rooms contains 576 and the parents room 1152 cubic feet, which is a much larger allowance than usual.

3rd By the use of Pearce's Cottage grate, the Girls Rooms are sufficiently heated & ventilated by the fire in the Washhouse.

Design No 2.

Front Elevation.

Side Elevation.

Scale ⅛ of an Inch to a Foot.

The winning design for cottages for agricultural labourers submitted to the Chard, Crewkerne, and Ilminster Labourers' Friend Society in 1857.

occupied by a copyholder. Much depended on the landlords. The cottages at Stoke St Gregory belonging to the Dean and Chapter of Wells were in a very bad condition but many landlords such as Lord Portman, Sir Alexander Hood at St Audries and Berkeley Napier at East Pennard, were beginning to build new model cottages for their tenants.

*

The Rev. John Poole, founder of Enmore School

By 1867 education, or rather the lack of it, was considered by many to be an important issue. The provision of rural education in Somerset was as varied as was agricultural practice and depended equally on landowners, benevolent gentry and the clergy. There were schools established across the county in the 1700s at, for example, East Harptree, Crowcombe, Spaxton and Dulverton, and by 1818 there were over nine hundred schools in Somerset – endowed, day and Sunday schools, supported by local subscribers, fees and grants from the national educational societies. In 1810 the Rev. John Poole established an avant garde monitorial system in his new school at Enmore, one of the first to provide free education, but this was unusual and most schools remained fee-paying – a penny a week – under the care of good-hearted but ill-trained teachers.

There must have been an early smattering of education for most of Somerset's children in the first half of the century and by the 1860s nearly all the men and women working on the Luttrell estates could fill in their week's work voucher and sign their names – but many were concerned that once children reached an age when they could work their attendance became sporadic and in the weeks spent in the fields they soon forgot all they had learned. Night schools in some parishes were well-attended by young men and women but there were still those who feared that if over-educated, agricultural labourers would get ideas above their station. 'Boys can learn quite enough from five to ten years of age,' said one Minehead clergyman.

Miss Munday and the pupils of Staple Fitzpaine School, c 1885

The 1872 Education Act brought in education for all, but school log books show that farming still ruled and whenever they were needed the children left to help in the fields. Perhaps the introduction of education in agriculture, encouraged by the Bath and West Society and a handful of landed gentry, was the best step forward for those looking for progress in the countryside into the next century.

THE AGE OF IMPROVEMENT

8

THE AGE OF IMPROVEMENT

Sue Berry

The period between 1750 and 1900 brought change to Somerset more rapidly than ever before. The county acquired new turnpike roads, canals and railways; its towns expanded to accommodate growing populations; and its people benefited from new forms of government, better policing and great advances in public health.

Perhaps nothing was more important in making possible this period of transformation than the rapid improvement in the county's roads. Since the sixteenth century the maintenance of Somerset roads had depended chiefly on the efforts of unpaid parish officials, and even in the eighteenth century the condition of minor roads remained notoriously bad: in 1785, for example, roads in Oake

Notice issued by the trustees of the Bath turnpike roads, c 1820.

THE TRUSTEES

OF THE

Bath Turnpike-Roads

HEREBY GIVE NOTICE,

THAT the Owner of any Waggon, Cart, or other Carriage of Burthen, who shall suffer any such Carriage to travel on the said Turnpike-Roads, *without his or her Christian and Surname, and Place of Abode, being painted thereon,* in large legible Letters, *on the Front or Off-Side of the same,* or shall draw the same with an illegal Number of Horses,* shall be fined according to Act of Parliament.

Opening of the Glastonbury Canal in 1832. The occasion was enlivened by the band which can be seen in the final barge.

parish were reported to be 'hardly passable' in winter, while at Hillfarrance they were 'narrow, rough, deep, stony and watery, and without any direction posts'. By contrast, the condition of major roads improved dramatically with the introduction of the turnpike road system in the early eighteenth century. The Bath Turnpike Trust was created in 1707, and by 1775 sixteen trusts had been established, including the Black Dog or Frome, Yeovil and Wincanton trusts in the east of the county, the Ilminster and Chard trusts in the south and the Minehead trust in the west. Tolls were levied on the users of the turnpikes, and the money raised was spent on widening, straightening, draining and diverting the roads.

In many areas it remained easier and more economical to transport heavy goods by river, and later by canal. The Conservators of the River Tone were established in 1699 to maintain the Tone in a navigable state at all times of the year and charged tolls to raise money for the essential work of scouring the river bed and maintaining the banks: as early as 1708 limeburners in two Devon parishes complained that a proposed increase in tolls would ruin their trade. By the late eighteenth century, astute businessmen saw in the development of canals not only a way of carrying goods cheaply but also, by investing in the building of the canals, a way of making a profit over and above the income from trade. Construction of the Somersetshire Coal Canal was authorised in 1794 for carrying the output of the mines at Radstock, Writhlington, Wellow and Timsbury to the Kennet and Avon Canal, thus opening up a large market for Somerset coal: as late as 1864 the coal canal was carrying over 155,000 tons of coal a year. The Bridgwater and Taunton Canal opened in 1827 as part of a grandiose, but unrealised, scheme for a continuous waterway joining the English Channel and the Bristol Channel. The Glastonbury Canal was completed in 1832, to be followed by the Westport Canal in 1840 and the Chard Canal in 1842.

Just as the canals had in many cases taken over the trade formerly carried by river, so the railways were in turn to supersede the canals. Isambard Kingdom Brunel, the engineer for the Bristol and Exeter Railway, was at Taunton in July 1842 to see the first passenger train arrive there. Eleven years later Langport Corporation gave a dinner to celebrate the arrival of the railway at their town. In his speech the mayor compared the hazards of travelling to London by the old North Devon coach, which took over 18 hours, with the speed and convenience of the train, which allowed travellers to 'take their breakfast at home, go to London, transact their business, and be home again in the evening'. He added that 'where railways went, there would commerce and intellect go too.' The opening of the Somerset Central Railway from Highbridge to Glastonbury in 1854 was celebrated with a procession through the ruins of Glastonbury Abbey, a lunch for nearly 1300 people and speeches by, among others, the mayor, the high sheriff and the bishop. The only cautionary note was struck by the inhabitants of Glastonbury who petitioned the directors of the railway company 'praying that they would not allow the quiet of the town to be disturbed by excursion-trains.' Others, as well, were not immediately persuaded by the speed and convenience of rail travel. Martha Vickery, an elderly inhabitant of Ilminster, was so appalled by her trip from Taunton to Bridgwater in 1855 that she flatly refused to make the return journey by train, explaining that instead she 'commed up in the coal boat sa far as Westport an then I walk'd home'.

The availability of speedy and comparatively inexpensive travel was one of the factors which led to the rise of mass tourism in the nineteenth century. Before the advent of the railways, travel for pleasure had in general been the prerogative of the gentry and the middle classes. In 1810, for example, members of the Esdaile family of Cothelstone made an excursion into West Somerset where they spent the night at Minehead – a 'miserable place' – and visited Dunster Castle, a sight which they considered should 'by no means be *miss'd by the traveller*'. It is true that Weston super Mare had already begun its development as a seaside resort before the arrival of the railway in 1841, a guide book of 1822 mentioning hotels and houses to rent for the season as well as jaunting cars, wheel and sedan

A train carrying livestock on the Great Western Railway at Kelston Bridge near Bath, c 1845.

Weston super Mare and the Knightstone baths, by S.C. Jones, c 1850. In the distance bathing machines put to sea.

Paddling at Burnham on Sea, c 1910.

chairs, ponies and donkeys which could be hired. But it was the railway above all which turned Burnham on Sea, Highbridge and Minehead into towns where tourism provided a vital new source of income. With the coming of the railways the travellers themselves included a far broader range of society, two disgruntled vistors from Birmingham in the early twentieth century describing the Cliffe Hotel at Cheddar as 'a day trippers rendevous', and Wells as 'a place fit only for old ladies of both sexes'.

The effect of the railways on the industries of Somerset was profound. Railways enabled farmers to import new machinery and breeds of animal which in turned led to increased production and the growth of an export trade.

Strawberries from the market gardens around Cheddar, whortleberries from the Quantock Hills and even primroses for the Conservative Party's Primrose Day were picked, packed and despatched to London by train. Local nurserymen such as Scott's of Merriott and Kelway's of Langport found that they now had easy access to a national market. So too did the products of industries such as the brick and tile works at Bridgwater, the glassworks at Nailsea, the stone quarries at Doulting and in the neighbourhood of Bath, the lead mines of the Mendip Hills and the iron mines of the Brendons, as well as the leather products of Clark's of Street, the canvas and sailcloth of Hayward's of Crewkerne, the horse-hair merchandise of Castle Cary, the iron wares of Singer's of Frome and the woollen goods of Fox Brothers of Wellington.

Access to a national market led in many cases to the decline and, in some instances, disappearance of the weekly markets and annual fairs which had been a feature of so many small towns in Somerset. In 1729 there were 180 annual fairs in the county. Two hundred years later scarcely more than thirty survived, such as those at Frome, Priddy, Wells, Yeovil and Crewkerne. In the 1870s Crewkerne fair was one of the largest in Somerset 'and so far as the pleasure side of it was concerned, there was nothing in the county to beat it.' The 'pleasure side' was always important. In 1819 the new Waterloo Fair at Wellington was opposed by those who regarded it as little more than an opportunity for drunkenness, debauchery and crime.

*

Many Somerset towns were transformed in the eighteenth and nineteenth centuries, not least by the building of 'genteel' accommodation to satisfy growing middle class demand. Bath's re-creation of itself from the early eighteenth century onward produced architecture of international significance. But more modest developments also took place, including Castle Street, Bridgwater (1723), Hammet Street, Taunton (1788), and, at a later period, such ambitious schemes as Oriel Terrace and Royal Crescent, Weston super Mare (1847). There were also some fine individual town houses, of which the Lions in Bridgwater (c 1730) is one striking early example. Increasing working-class populations were no less in need of accommodation. The rapid growth of Frome as a centre of cloth manufacture during the late seventeenth and eighteenth centuries led to the development of the remarkable Trinity area of the town: there, in the eighteenth century, lived cardmakers, broadweavers and wiredrawers. Some employers, such as John Lucas, the owner of the Nailsea Glassworks, built

The shambles in the Market Place at Shepton Mallet, c 1895, with the Bunch of Grapes Inn and the British Workman, possibly refreshment rooms, in the background.

Waterloo Fair.

WHILE strenuous exertions are making to add one more to the already too numerous temptations to drunkenness and riot, it is certainly the duty of every one, disapproving such scenes, to oppose it.

The establishment of WATERLOO FAIR can have no other effect, than to entice the industrious Labourer and Mechanic from his employment, to spend his hard earned wages in self-gratification, while in many instances his wife and family are in want of necessary food, or at best, dependent on the precarious and debasing supply of parochial relief, for the means of existence.

POOR MAN! consider what you lose by excess and drunkenness; not only the time you sacrifice and the money you spend, but what is of much greater importance, you undermine your strength, and destroy your health; you incur the displeasure of the God that will judge you.

RICH MAN! consider what you do, by encouraging such scenes; the Poor Rates are increased, the health and morals of the people are injured, and God is openly blasphemed.

CHERRY, PRINTER, WELLINGTON.

Notice urging opposition to the holding of Waterloo Fair, Wellington, 1819.

houses for their employees. In the 1840s, Taunton's rapid expansion led to the creation of 'almost a new town' for working-class inhabitants in the area around the union workhouse.

Behind an increasingly well-built facade, however, Somerset towns often struggled to improve the living conditions of their inhabitants. In the 1840s, a government report recorded that at Frome 'no sewerage deserving the name exists', and at Taunton sanitary conditions were evidently no better. Various bodies were established to improve the condition of towns. In some places turnpike trustees, already responsible for main roads, took on the additional duties of lighting, paving and drainage. Thus, in 1857, it was to the Wells Turnpike Commissioners that the bishop of the diocese addressed his complaint about the noxious smells which wafted from an open drain 'into the doorways and windows of the palace by every south and south west wind'. The inhabitants of Wells St Cuthbert, for their part, approached the commissioners to ask for more street lamps in part of High Street, 'it being so extremely dark'.

In 1830 Yeovil became one of the Somerset towns which established a body of Improvement Commissioners, but real progress in improving urban conditions was generally delayed until the establishment of a central Board of Health in 1848. The Board had powers to create local boards where ten per cent of the population voted for one. Taunton was the first town in Somerset to take advan-

tage of the new regulations, despite the opposition of the Market Trustees who had been the town's *de facto* government since 1792, and Burnham and Clevedon followed soon after. By 1870 Weston super Mare had instituted a scavenging or rubbish collection service, although many inhabitants failed to take advantage of it. Instead, refuse and dung were allowed to accumulate 'until they contaminate the air around and become injurious to public health'. The reason for reluctance to use the service, it was said, was that by saving the rubbish in back yards and outhouses it could be sold to private hauliers for a few pence.

Hammet Street, Taunton, seen from Church Square, c 1800. The street was built in 1788 at the instigation of Sir Benjamin Hammet, Taunton's MP.

Despite the founding of dispensaries and hospitals, it was little wonder that insanitary conditions meant that disease was widespread and death rates were high during much of the eighteenth and nineteenth centuries. In 1721 Lady Mary Wortley Montagu was given permission to test smallpox inoculation on seven condemned criminals and the following year two members of the royal family were inoculated. The practice was rapidly taken up by the gentry and in 1752 Julia Trevelyan wrote from Wells to her father-in-law at Nettlecombe asking permission for her son to be inoculated. 'I have an opinion of Inoculation, as being far less dangerous, than having the Small-Pox in the natural way,' she writes. Her optimism was not always borne out by experience. The vicar of Shepton Mallet noted in 1821 that six of his flock had died of smallpox, 'three of them from *innoculation*'. But without inoculation the ravages of the disease were even worse. Of the twenty-eight people buried in the parish of Blagdon in 1777, seventeen had died of small pox which was introduced into the parish when a corpse was brought from a distance for burial. 'A most barbarous Custom!' a note in the parish register records, 'which the Rector has since entirely prohibited and recommends the same to his Successor.' Unfortunately, however, the very same thing happened again in 1783.

Childhood diseases – scarlatina, measles, whooping cough – were still causing many deaths well into the late nineteenth and early twentieth centuries. The headmistress of Ilchester School recorded on 10 June 1874 that 'Harry Evans died Friday and Amelia Sansom yesterday of fever,' and in the weeks ahead four more pupils also fell victim. Twenty years later the Kilver Street School in Shepton

Mallet was closed 'by order of the Managers on account of the prevalence of Scarlet Fever in the district'. Cholera was another scourge that appeared periodically, 1849 being a particularly bad year. In August the committee of Bridgwater Infirmary issued a notice to 'all poor persons not entitled to Medical Relief from the Medical Officer of the Bridgwater Union' offering free help and advice 'in all cases of bowel complaints'. In October, after six deaths had occurred in Monmouth Street, some of the children who lived there were taken into the workhouse to protect them from infection. In December, after the threat of the disease had faded, it was noted that the outbreak had considerably increased expenses 'by causing an addition of upwards of 1000 patients beyond the average number.' In some Somerset communities tradesmen and artisans formed medical clubs to help themselves if they fell ill: the rules of the Chewton Mendip club, dated 1836, state that members had to 'furnish their own bottles and bandages, and in cases of rupture, their own trusses', while the rules of the Montacute, Stoke and Odcombe club, c 1878, provide that the surgeon elected must supply all sick members with attendance and medicine except in the cases of childbirth and venereal disease. Other poor people relied on such remedies as they could find, including the patent medicines available from local chemists. Keeble's of Crewkerne, the 'cheapest chemist in England', could supply a remarkable Life Tonic which promised relief from symptoms including weakness, depression, nervous debility, brain fag, nervous dyspepsia, and sleeplessness.

Water-borne diseases such as cholera and typhoid could never effectively be prevented so long as drinking water was drawn from wells, streams or rivers contaminated by the leakage of sewerage from cess pits and privies. In 1872 Wincanton Rural Sanitary Authority appointed an Inspector of Public Nuisances and resolved that where privies drained into cesspits these must be covered over and that no drainage of any house or yard should be allowed to flow into the public street. Two years later the authority sought tenders for building a reservoir at Penselwood, supplying iron pipes to be delivered at the railway station, laying the pipes and supplying and laying sewer pipes and building settling

Advertisement, c 1890, issued by Keeble's of Crewkerne who claimed to be 'the cheapest chemist in England'.

tanks. In the same period other Somerset towns were also benefiting for the first time from sewage treatment plants and from supplies of piped, filtered water. But even the arrival of a piped water system did not guarantee a constant supply. In 1865 it is recorded that the water supply at Taunton was turned off at noon until the following morning, leading to complaints that the stench from the urinals at Castle Green was frequently so great that 'it was with difficulty anyone could remain in them for the purpose for which they had been erected.' A continuous water supply only reached Taunton in 1878 with the opening of the Blagdon Hill reservoir.

*

Somerset's towns were faced not only with the increasing challenge of ensuring public health in the eighteenth and nineteenth centuries but with problems concerning the prevention, detection and prosecution of crime. It is clear that the medieval system of annually elected, unpaid parish constables could no longer cope with the demands being made on it. Some idea of the difficulties faced by the constables can be found in the diary of Isaac Gregory, parish constable of Frome in 1817–18. Most of the entries relate to cases of drunkenness and minor theft as well as to domestic disputes. Called to the Ship Inn, where one of the customers had had his pocket picked, Gregory broke up the quarrelsome gathering at the landlord's request, and was 'much grieved to find one of the company was in my class at the Chapel School when I was teacher there'. On Sundays Gregory seems to have spent his time strolling round the town looking for 'idle boys' who should have been at church or chapel. The parish constable's jurisdiction ended at the parish boundary, making it very difficult to follow up a crime, or for sufficient men to be gathered together to deal with public disorder. In some cases local inhabitants called upon the military for assistance: in 1795 a petition signed by many of the more prominent men of the Hundred of Wellow demanded that 'a Military Force of Infantry be immediately furnished to act as an internal Guard' for a manufactory that had been threatened with destruction. At other times, as during agricultural disturbances in 1830, special constables were sworn in and issued with staves or clubs. Land owners formed associations which offered rewards for information leading to the conviction of offenders: in 1837 the Camel, Cadbury and Sparkford Association for the Protection of

Cheap Street, Frome, c 1910.

Property and the Prosecution of Offenders issued a notice. They would pay a £10 reward for conviction in cases of murder, arson, burglary and highway robbery, and lesser amounts in cases of maiming cattle, stealing hay or poultry, cutting trees or breaking hedges. The notice also listed the punishments for those found guilty of certain offences; in that troubled decade, the sentence for arson was death.

The Municipal Corporations Act, 1835, established watch committees in 178 boroughs throughout the country, allowing the employment of constables paid for through the rates. Four years later the County Police Act enabled the Justices of the Peace to maintain a paid police force if they wished, and in 1856 the County and Borough Police Act was passed. Under this legislation Somerset established a county police force in the same year, its personnel consisting of a chief constable, his deputy, four superintendents, twelve inspectors, or second-class superintendents, twenty sergeants, ninety first class constables and 132 second class constables. Some boroughs such as Glastonbury, Wells and Yeovil were happy to give up control of their own forces and amalgamate with the county force, but others were not. Chard did not do so until 1889 when obliged to by legislation. On its creation the Chard force had been provided with three pairs of handcuffs, one pair of leg irons, three staves, three cutlasses, three dark lanterns and three leathern waist belts. It was never the most efficient of forces: in 1850 a prisoner escaped from custody because the cells were insecure and in 1855 Superintendent Elms was censured for having allowed another prisoner to escape, for letting one of the constables live out of the police house and for having taken in a lodger at the station.

Although death was the prescribed penalty for many crimes, in practice the sentence was often commuted to transportation. The American colonies had received transportees from the seventeenth century onwards, but the outbreak of the American War of Independence in 1776 brought that traffic to an end. In 1787, the 'First Fleet' sailed for Australia, carrying with it at least three Somerset women convicted of theft at various places in the county. Transportation to Australia continued until 1868 and the fate of transported convicts, and their life in Australia, fascinated the law-abiding population. In 1847 a lecture given at the Poulett Arms in Chard was entitled 'Fourteen Years Transportation: The Life Of A Convict' in which the lecturer appeared in the 'convict's dress, chains, etc, as worn in Norfolk Island'. Parents and guardians of youth were earnestly requested to attend. Executions, carried out in public until 1868, were a prime source of entertainment for many of the population. When Thomas Nation of

View of Fore Street, Chard, in the late eighteenth century.

Wiveliscome was executed in April 1857, the *Taunton Courier* reported that the grounds of Shire Hall were thrown open to the public, some people arriving before daybreak to be certain of a place:

'Residents from Wiveliscome, Huish Champflower, Stogumber, Upton, Dunster, Milverton, Bishop's Lydeard, Clatworthy, Skilgate, Monksilver, Williton, Chipstable, Raddington, Nettlecombe and Wellington predominated, but nearly all the surrounding villages sent some members of the rustic population, either mounted or on foot, to witness the appalling spectacle. '

In 1883, when executions were carried out behind the prison walls, the head-master of a Taunton school recorded that the number of boys present was smaller than usual 'partly owing to two murderers ... being hanged at the gaol.'

For those lucky enough to escape both execution and transportation, there remained the county's three gaols at Ilchester, Shepton Mallet and Wilton, near Taunton. According to Henry 'Orator' Hunt, writing in 1821, conditions at Ilchester varied from the excesses enjoyed by prisoners who were in favour with the governor, William Bridle, to the existence endured by one James Hillier: he was manacled so severely for nine days and nights that when the turnkeys came to remove his chains 'the iron rings thereof were almost buried in his flesh and ... they were obliged to use considerable force and violence to get them out of the flesh.'

*

At the close of the Victorian period, the living and working conditions of Somerset people had improved to an extent which would have seemed impossible to their ancestors in 1750. Although hardship and poverty still existed in the towns which had grown so rapidly during this period, the progress brought about by advances in medical science, the rapid and easy transport of goods and improvements in housing and sanitation meant that the majority of the population looked forward with hope and confidence to the twentieth century.

Illustration from Henry Hunt's pamphlet A Peep into a Prison *or, the Inside of Ilchester Bastille, 1821, describing conditions in the gaol.*

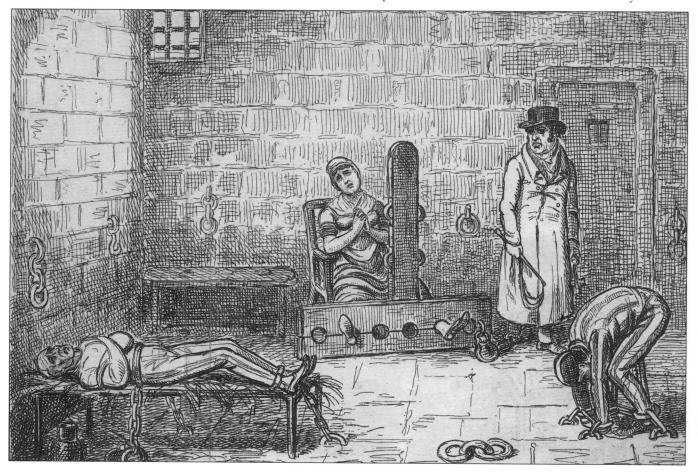

MODERN TIMES

9

MODERN TIMES

Tom Mayberry

In towns and villages throughout Great Britain one event dominated the midsummer of 1897. Queen Victoria, who had reigned more years than most people had been alive, was celebrating her Diamond Jubilee, and a thankful nation celebrated with her. Work stopped, and the preparations of local committees were brought to fulfilment in processions and church services, Jubilee dinners and streets decked with flags. Children in their thousands received commemorative medals, and countless speeches delivered by local dignitaries expressed the popular mood. Throughout Somerset on Jubilee Day, 22 June, festivities were concluded by the lighting of bonfires which shone out on a warm summer evening from Dunkery Beacon to Timsbury Sleight. Ninety-seven bonfires were counted from the Poldens above Shapwick, and from Cothelstone Hill near Taunton more than a hundred were visible.

Those celebrations – recorded by sepia photographs and in the columns of the local press – have often been thought of as the last act of a dying era, a vivid, carefree moment before the face of rural England was transformed. In reality, the process of transformation was already far-advanced by the time the bonfires blazed in 1897. After the first wave of rural emigration in the 1830s and '40s a second had gathered strength by the late 1860s. From villages south of Taunton

Children at a Wellington school photographed for the Diamond Jubilee of Queen Victoria, 1897.

a 'great migration' was reported in 1869 as labourers and their families abandoned the countryside seeking more plentiful and better-paid work, often in Somerset towns, in South Wales, or in the North. During the same period increasing numbers were also following the first generation of emigrants who had left the shores of England altogether. Though the number of inhabitants in the county almost doubled between 1801 and 1901, it was overwhelmingly Somerset's larger towns which experienced growth: Yeovil's population increased from 2,774 in 1801 to 11,704 a century later, and Taunton's from 5,794 to 19,535, while in the special case of Weston super Mare a population of 138 grew to a remarkable 18,275. By contrast, the slow depopulation of rural areas seemed inexorable. 'Many families have left the neighbourhood,' the headmistress of Thurlbear School wrote in January 1900; and the following year: 'children still are leaving the parish.'

Retreat from the countryside was attributed by many to increasing dependence on farm machinery and to the farming depression which affected English agriculture after 1878: a run of wet summers and an influx of foreign grain, together with refrigerated meat imports from New Zealand and Argentina, severely affected agricultural profits as well as the ability of farmers to employ labour. When Rider Haggard visited Somerset in 1902, he found other reasons for depopulation as well. At Williton he was told that elementary education had made rural labourers impatient with their lives so that they longed for the 'glare and company of the towns'. Nor were they content any longer to survive on 12s a week, a North Petherton farmer explained, when others who had left for the Welsh coalfields could earn far more, though at far greater risk. Increasingly, the cry of 'back to the land' went unheeded, and between 1881 and 1901 the number of agricultural labourers in Somerset fell by 39% from 28,141 to 17,234.

Recruits at Tatworth, near Chard, going off to war, 1914.

Despite a dwindling labour supply, Somerset farmers survived agricultural depression better than those in mainly arable counties to the east. By the beginning of the century Somerset's farming landscape was so much dominated by dairying and stock-rearing that 77% of farmland was permanent grass, and included pasture for a quarter of a million cattle and about half a million sheep. Few farms were over 300 acres in extent, the average for the county as a whole

being about 60 acres. The modest holdings of small tenant farmers were often the most vulnerable to economic pressures. In the dairying districts of North Somerset, for example, the advent of refrigerated transport drove down the price of milk and forced some long-established dairy farmers to give up their farms. 'At one time,' Eldred Walker wrote in 1906, 'these farms were handed down like heirlooms from father to son. Now the holdings frequently pass to fresh tenants, and the old names are known no more.'

Unveiling of the war memorial outside St Mary's Church, Taunton, 1920.

*

A rainy Bank Holiday marked the arrival of war on Monday, 4 August 1914. On the esplanade at Watchet blindfold boxing, beauty contests for both sexes, and bun and treacle competitions were held in defiance both of bad weather and rumours of war, while at Bristol, Somerset were heading for a one-wicket defeat at the hands of Gloucestershire. On Tuesday, 5 August, Lord St Audries spoke at Bagborough of 'the gravest crisis this country had known for one hundred years', and by the end of the week Somerset men aged between 17 and 25 were already being urged to enlist. In the following weeks recruiting meetings were held throughout the county, one of the most memorable taking place in Bridgwater on the opening day of St Matthew's Fair, 30 September. A 'huge concourse' gathered in the fair field to hear an address from Colonel H.B. Patton, commander of the Somerset National Reserve Brigade, and by the time the meeting closed with the playing of the National Anthem many men had volunteered. Throughout the county the number of recruits was enormous – it included 3,500 men from Taunton alone – and when the war ended the terrible reckoning showed that more than 8,000 had lost their lives (about 10% of Somerset's male population between the ages of 15 and 39, and about 13% of those who served).

Though the First World War left Somerset farmers desperate for labour, their fortunes rose quickly as they answered the government's demands for more wheat. Between 1914 and 1919 over 34,000 acres of permanent grass were ploughed up in the county, chiefly to grow cereals to feed the nation. Under the direction of the county's War Agricultural Committee, 136 tractors and 372 horses were acquired to boost agricultural production, and by the end of the war farmers felt justified in hoping that the hard times were finally gone. But such

Albert Payne at Badger Street Farm, Thurlbear, c 1930.

hopes were soon disappointed. A post-war boom was followed at the end of 1921 by economic collapse in which Somerset farmers suffered greatly. In March 1922, a group of them petitioned the County Council's Smallholdings Committee, seeking to be excused the Lady Day rents which were about to fall due:

'The last season has been for us a disaster...you are aware that the market value of our live-stock has fallen to less than half what we paid for it, that the price of corn has dropped since we planted it to almost a pre-war level, and implements which we purchased at exorbitant prices are now almost valueless. We have, many of us, nothing to carry on with next year, very little value left in our stock, no possibility of borrowing money, no money to plant with, and no money to pay our rents with or even to live upon our holdings.'

A partial recovery was quickly followed by a return to depression in the later 1920s. By 1932 some 43,000 acres of farmland had been abandoned since the end of the war; and when in 1931 the Bishop's Lydeard and District Agricultural Association tried to arrange a ploughing match, there were only two remaining arable fields in the whole area to choose from. That year, the newly-elected National Government promised tariffs to protect English agriculture from the ruinous effects of foreign competition. But it was only with the outbreak of another world war that Somerset farmers recovered their prosperity and pride.

Farmers were not alone in suffering the effects of economic depression. The falling value of land and rental income also dramatically undermined the posi-

tion of Somerset landowners, as did the introduction of Estate Duty in 1894. In 1883, 108 landowners owned 43% of the whole area of the county, the greatest of them, Viscount Portman, having a Somerset estate of more than 24,000 acres. The Portman mansion at Bryanston in Dorset remains one of England's most overwhelming expressions of late-Victorian wealth, and Somerset too acquired some grandiose houses in the second half of the nineteenth century: the Tudor gothic mansion of the Acland-Hoods, for example, was completed at St Audries in about 1870, and at Wraxall the vast mansion of the Gibbs family, Tyntesfield, acquired a chapel of 'astonishing size' in 1875. By 1900, however, the great days were coming to an end as the financial returns from agricultural estates fell ever lower, and in the period immediately before and after the First World War many estates were broken up and sold. The Marston estate of the Earls of Cork and Orrery went in 1905, the Thring family lands at Alford in 1906, the Sandhill estate of the Lethbridges in 1913, and the Weston super Mare lands of the Smyth-Pigotts in 1914. The period 1918 to 1922 saw the break-up of estates such as those belonging to the Dukes of Devonshire, the Wingfield Digbys, and Lord de Mauley, as well as others centred on Shapwick, Over Stowey and Donyatt; and after a long attrition, the remaining Portman lands in Somerset were finally sold to the Crown in 1944 to meet an enormous bill for death duties. As examples of land redistribution these sales were probably without parallel since the dissolution of the monasteries, and allowed at least some tenant farmers to purchase the holdings on which they had worked so long and so unprofitably.

*

While the old order was fast going to decay, new and more democratic forms of government were being introduced, especially at county level. Somerset's unelected JPs had for centuries been responsible not only for dispensing justice but for administering many other aspects of life. In 1888, however, the Local Government Act provided for elected county councils to take over the administrative role of the justices, and on 31 January 1889, in the setting of Highbridge Town Hall, Somerset County Council met for the first time. Sir Richard Horner Paget was in the chair, one indication that the Somerset gentry still expected to

The Hon. E.W.B. Portman (1856–1911), eldest son and heir of the 2nd Viscount Portman, being carried in an estate wagon from Hestercombe House for burial at Cheddon Fitzpaine. He caught a chill while playing golf and died soon after.

County Hall, Taunton, in 1936, the year after it was opened as the new headquarters of Somerset County Council. Before that date the council's offices were chiefly in Weston super Mare.

control and lead, even though the new council also included men such as the boot and shoe manufacturer W.S. Clark of Street, and Samuel Kidner, a well-known Milverton farmer. The city of Bath became a county borough as part of the same reforms, and in 1894 further legislation led to the setting up of district and parish councils.

In the course of fifty years Somerset County Council assumed a range of duties far exceeding those the justices had performed. From the beginning it was responsible for mental health provision, opening a vast new mental hospital at

Cotford, near Taunton, in 1897. The council became Somerset's Education Authority in 1902 and built scores of new schools, including a splendid art deco secondary school at Weston super Mare. In 1930 it took over administration of the Poor Law, renaming the hated workhouses 'Public Assistance Institutions' and providing in them, so it was claimed, 'homely and comfortable quarters for the aged and infirm'. And as local authority for a chiefly rural county it acquired an extensive farm estate – amounting in 1939 to more than 21,000 acres – which provided smallholdings for ex-servicemen and others as a gateway into agriculture.

But nothing made greater demands on County resources than the maintenance of Somerset's roads, a duty which was shared with district councils. Roads which had served the age of the pony and trap were soon found to be inadequate for motor cars, the first three of which (Y1, Y2 and Y3) were registered to Arthur Thring of Sutton Montis in November 1903. Though the stone-breaker with his pile of flints remained a familiar sight at Somerset roadsides as late as the 1920s, tar dressing – first tried at Minehead in 1908 – was soon universal, while on major routes such as the A38 gangs of workmen began widening and straightening what a quieter age had been content to leave narrow and crooked. The rise of the motor car made road improvements inevitable: by August 1938 the A38 at Bradford on Tone carried a daily average of 4,408 vehicles between six in the morning and ten at night, and dramatic increases in traffic lay ahead.

*

The advantages of greater mobility were not confined to people such as Arthur Thring, cutting a dash in his blue and black seven horsepower Benz. 'Bicycles galore' were said to have filled the streets of Williton during the inter-war years – as they did the streets of every Somerset town – and offered a degree of mobility and independence unimagined by earlier generations. So too did the charabanc and motor bus. 'Everyone walked everywhere until the 1930s,' a resident of Marston Bigot recalled, 'when an old-type charabanc christened the "Red Robin" came into use.' In Taunton during the same period Edwin Smith ran a charabanc called 'The Rambler' to Sidmouth once a week, stopping at villages along the way to collect passengers; and at Alcombe an open-sided bus nicknamed 'The Toast Rack' took passengers to Minehead for a penny. The charabanc was important not only for the ordinary journeys of life but also for the annual

Road mending at South Petherton in about 1905. The contractors are the Baker family.

A charabanc outing from Hambridge, c 1930.

seaside excursions which by the 1930s had become a central part of childhood experience. At South Petherton, children from the Congregational Sunday School, with 'parents, grandparents, aunts and uncles', would regularly fill nine or ten charabancs and set out for Weymouth, Weston or Burnham on Sea, arriving home at night 'very tired but gloriously happy' after the best day of the year.

Just as memorable as summer days at the seaside were the newly-discovered wonders of the cinema. In the early 1930s silent cowboy films were frequent attractions for forty or fifty rowdy children in the Methodist schoolroom at South Petherton, where the long-suffering projectionist, Fred Allen, struggled to keep control. 'When the noise became unbearable, usually from the boys, who always sat at the back, Mr Allen would stop the film and threaten not to start it again unless we behaved.' There were already 25 commercial cinemas in Somerset by 1927, including the Beau Nash in Bath and the Cosy Cinema in Minehead, and by 1939 there were no fewer than 43, of which Weston super Mare's art deco Odeon, by Cecil Howitt, was among the most ambitious. Public libraries and swimming baths also added to the facilities towns could offer by the 1930s, and the building of new houses, especially in urban areas, was bringing an unfamiliar degree of comfort to the lives of many people. Council houses, such as those on the Lyngford and Lambrook estates at Taunton, began to appear in the decade after the First World War, and by 1935 a boom in private house-building was also underway. The middle-class houses so familiar from that period – brick-built, semi-detached, bow-windowed and dependable – remain some of the most enduring parts of the Somerset housing stock, and reflect a society which, after long years of economic struggle and on the brink of another war, was at last recovering its confidence and its strength.

*

The Second World War profoundly affected Somerset. While thousands departed for distant battlefields, the lives of those who remained at home were transformed by rationing and the blackout, evacuees and Land Army girls, American soldiers and Home Guard patrols. Even before Mr Chamberlain's announcement of war on 3 September 1939, preparations in the county were far advanced. Somerset farmers, as in 1914, had ploughed up grassland in order to grow more crops, and had soon added 48,000 acres to the area of Somerset's arable land (much more would follow). In June 1938 Civil Defence preparations began when the county was divided into eight ARP areas. And in the weeks before war was declared Helen Orr-Ewing was enrolling members into the Women's Voluntary Service and setting up branches in towns and rural areas throughout Somerset. It was the arrival of evacuees on a September weekend in 1939 which was for most Somerset people the bewildering proof that Britain was indeed at war again. Thousands of children, many with their mothers, reached Somerset by train on 2–3 September and were billeted on households both in the towns and the country. Weston and the area around received over 10,000 evacuees on those two days, the Taunton area almost 4,000, the Borough of Yeovil 2,500, and other parts of the county many thousands more. In the following year there was a second wave of arrivals when fears of invasion led to the evacuation of towns on the south coast. Land Army Girls also began to appear, digging for victory on the county's enormously increased arable acreages. There were 454 Land Army Girls in Somerset at the end of 1941, no fewer than 1,793 two years later.

It was a period of intense activity. In the summer of 1941 stop lines, consisting of massively-constructed pill-boxes, appeared in the landscape; and in the same months Somerset men were flocking to join the newly-created Home Guard (briefly known as the Local Defence Volunteers), a force which was eventually 24,000 strong. Signposts were removed, barricades appeared at the entrances to towns and villages, and every night Home Guard patrols would listen as enemy bombers flew high overhead on their way to Bristol, South Wales or the Midlands. Somerset itself did not escape enemy action, and in the course of the war more than 60,000 bombs fell on the county, most of them dropped randomly in open countryside. There were also deliberate attacks, such as those over Yeovil in October 1940 when 35 people died in direct hits on two air-raid shelters and 13 service personnel were killed at Houndstone Camp.

Nothing, however, could have prepared Somerset for the Baedeker raids of 1942, Hitler's answer to the allied bombing of Lübeck and Rostock in March that year. Incensed that the medieval cities had been so badly damaged, he decided to launch even more devastating attacks on the historic cities of England, reput-

Members of the Women's Land Army at Wrington preparing for a victory parade through Bath at the end of the Second World War.

edly using the Baedeker tourist guide in selecting the targets. Exeter, Norwich, York and Canterbury all suffered severely. But nowhere did the raids cause more destruction than in Bath. On the nights of 25, 26 and 27 April, German planes flew low over the undefended city in the moonlight, dive-bombing its buildings and machine-gunning its streets. Thousands of buildings were damaged or destroyed and 417 people were killed. From the ruins of one house, the dead body of an airman was brought out, his arms still outstretched in a vain effort to save the life of his young daughter, and from around the city came other stories of tragedy and heroism. A few days after the raids, in the setting of the windswept Haycombe Cemetery, the bishop of the diocese and a great crowd of mourners gathered at mass graves to bury more than 250 of the victims. The last of the Baedeker raids took place on 28 and 29 June, when Weston super Mare was chosen as the unlikely target. Under the light of another full moon, German incendiaries and high explosives rained down, causing great damage to a wide area of the town and inflicting heavy casualties: a total of 400 people were injured in the Weston raids, and 102 lost their lives.

Somerset never again suffered so severely in the war, and its later experiences were dominated by the growing numbers of American troops who were based in the county during the long build-up to D Day. They began to arrive in the summer of 1942, and by the spring of 1944 Somerset was estimated to contain as many American as British inhabitants. Ammunition dumps appeared every-where; transporters bearing rescue launches, landing barges and steam tugs crowded the roads; and in the first hours of 6 June the aircraft navigation lights which filled the night sky confirmed that D Day had at last arrived. Though wounded American soldiers were soon brought back to Somerset for treatment in the six American General Hospitals the county contained, D Day effectively ended Somerset's war. On 3 December battalions of the Somerset Home Guard

King George VI and Queen Elizabeth visiting Bath following the Baedeker raids of April 1942.

held their stand-down parades in rain-soaked streets, and on 5 May 1945 the long-silent church bells welcomed VE Day. At Taunton, soldiers and civilians danced round the Parade, while at Bridgwater the inhabitants found their own special way to mark the return to peace. Having painted the dome of the Market House red, white and blue, they surged through the streets bearing an effigy of Hitler before them and threw it on a bonfire in St Matthew's Field.

*

The great stimulus to agriculture which war had provided was not followed by a farming slump as many had feared. Though arable acreages declined rapidly when the war ended, Somerset farmers looked to their strengths: by 1950 the county had become the leading milk producer in England, and its agricultural output as a whole was said to be worth over £27 million a year. Agriculture, it was reported in 1953, was 'obviously the most important county industry', a status made secure by the price guarantees introduced under the Agriculture Act in 1947. It was, however, by no means Somerset's only industry. At Frome, about 400 were employed in limestone quarrying, and others worked in the printing trade; the North Somerset coalfield, already far-advanced in decline, accounted for 3,400 workers, and Fry's chocolate factory at Keynsham for 2,500. At Street and Glastonbury the boot, shoe, and sheepskin factories of the Clark and Morland families were pre-eminent, while Wellington maintained its historic loyalty to woollen manufacture. The war had transformed the fortunes of the Westland Aircraft Company in Yeovil, as well as bringing part of Government chart-making activities to Taunton; and at Shepton Mallet in 1953 Francis Showering began national distribution of his new invention, Babycham. But just as important for employment in Somerset during the 1950s were the burgeoning service industries. Builders and decorators, workers in transport, communications and the utilities, public administrators and those who depended on the tourist trade all made up an increasing proportion of the workforce, a fact which pointed already to a future in which neither agriculture nor manufacturing would play the predominant part.

In the twenty years from 1951, the population of Somerset grew by almost 24% from 551,305 to 682,664, a larger increase than had occurred in the whole of the

The Somerset team in 1978, the year before they finally won the Gillette Cup. Back row: Keith Jennings, Hallam Moseley, Peter Roebuck, Joel Garner, Colin Dredge, Ian Botham, Vic Marks and Phil Slocombe. Front row: Neil Russom, Graham Burgess, Peter Denning, Brian Rose (captain), Derek Taylor, Viv Richards and Dennis Breakwell.

fifty preceding years. New houses were built in great numbers, public utilities at last came within reach of the majority of inhabitants, and the problems caused by rapid increases in road traffic called forth generally inadequate solutions. Only the completion in 1976 of the M5 motorway from Exeter to Carlisle at last freed towns such as Taunton, Bridgwater and Highbridge from complete domination by the motor car. But at the same time the M5 destroyed forever Somerset's rural isolation and opened the county to the influences of the greater world as never before: future generations may well conclude that, for good or ill, nothing changed Somerset more than the motorway.

It is certain at least that the last three decades of the twentieth century have transformed Somerset at bewildering speed. It lost its northern territory, including Weston super Mare, to the unloved county of Avon in 1974; and when Avon was abolished in 1996, new unitary authorities called 'North Somerset' and 'Bath and North East Somerset' were created, each with the status of a county. Road schemes, housing developments, and out-of-town superstores proliferated in the '80s and '90s, the physical consequences of which are plain to see on the outskirts of towns such as Taunton and Yeovil. But the effects of change, and of changing attitudes, have been felt most keenly in rural Somerset. Middle class wealth has altered the character of many villages, and antagonism between 'locals' and 'incomers' – an increasingly empty distinction – has sometimes been bitter. Mendip quarrying, gipsy sites, drainage and peat digging on the Levels, hunting with hounds, rights of way and the destruction of hedgerows have all aroused great controversy, a reflection of widely conflicting interests within an increasingly fragmented society. If there is consensus about anything it is that we have for too long taken the natural environment for granted: between 1936 and 1996, for example, 97% of Somerset's unimproved flower-rich grasslands were destroyed.

The Glastonbury Festival, Worthy Farm, Pilton, 1995. The festival, founded in 1970 by Michael and Jean Eavis, at first attracted an audience of 1,500. In 1998, 100,000 attended.

Somerset farmers, the traditional stewards of the countryside, find themselves in crisis as the century ends. Incomes have fallen dramatically in the face of fierce competition, oversupply, and concerns about food safety; the subsidies on which farming has depended since the war are no longer sufficient to guarantee

Sign of the times at Daw's Green, Trull, 1998.

a living; and the intensive farming methods encouraged by government policy for more than fifty years are increasingly criticised for their environmental effects. Even if predictions of widespread bankruptcies and abandoned farm-land are exaggerated, there seems little doubt that farming, and the life of the countryside, are reaching a turning-point.

How will the landscape of Somerset be cared for in the next generation? Can rural communities retain their sense of identity in a period of vastly increased mobility? Will Somerset survive at all as a unit of government and a focus of loyalty fifty years from now? On the brink of a new millennium the questions multiply. The answers are as yet very few.

SELECT BIBLIOGRAPHY

Alcock, Leslie, *et al.*, *Cadbury Castle, Somerset: the Early Medieval Archaeology* (1995)

Aston, Michael (ed.), *Aspects of the Medieval Landscape of Somerset* (1988)

Barnes, Thomas Garden, *Somerset, 1625–1640: A County's Government During the 'Personal Rule'* (1961)

Bettey, J.H., *Rural Life in Wessex*, 1500–1900 (1977)

Bettey, J.H., *Church & Community: the Parish Church in English Life* (1979)

Bettey, J.H., *Sacred & Satiric: Medieval Stone Carving in the West Country* (1982)

Billingsley, John, *General View of the Agriculture in the County of Somerset* (1797)

Bond, James, *Somerset Parks and Gardens: A Landscape History* (1998)

Bush, Robin, *Somerset: The Complete Guide* (1994)

Bushell, T.A., *Somerset on Guard* (Somerset County Gazette, Nov. 1950–Feb. 1951)

Clifton, Robin, *The Last Popular Rebellion: The Western Rising of 1685* (1984)

Collinson, Rev. John, *The History and Antiquities of Somerset* (3 vols, 1791)

Costen, Michael, *The Origins of Somerset* (1992)

Darby, H.C., and Finn, R. Welldon (eds), *The Domesday Geography of South-West England* (1967)

Dunning, Robert (ed.), *Christianity in Somerset* (1976)

Dunning, Robert, *Some Somerset Country Houses: A Personal Selection* (1991)

Dunning, R.W., *A History of Somerset* (1978)

Dunning, R.W., *The Monmouth Rebellion: a Complete Guide to the Rebellion* (1985)

Quaife, G.R., *Wanton Wenches and Wayward Wives* (1979)

Savage, Sir William, 'Somerset Towns', *Proceedings of the Somerset Archaeological and Natural History Society*, vol. 99/100, pp. 49–74 (1956)

Somerset Federation of Women's Institutes, *Somerset Within Living Memory* (1992)

Stuart-Menteath, T., *The Land of Britain: The Report of the Land Utilisation Survey of Briatin: Part 86, Somerset* (1938)

Thompson, W. Harding, *Somerset: Regional Survey* (1934)

Underdown, David, *Somerset in the Civil War and Interregnum* (1973)

Underdown, David, *Revel, Riot and Rebellion: Popular Politics and Culture in England, 1603–1660* (1985)

Victoria History of the County of Somerset, vols 1 (1906) and 2 (1911), ed. William Page, vols 3 (1974), 4 (1978), 5 (1985) and 6 (1992), ed. R.W. Dunning

Wickham, A.K., *Churches of Somerset* (1953, 1965)

Williams, Michael, *The Draining of the Somerset Levels* (1970)

INDEX

Figures in italics refer to illustration page numbers